PRACTICAL DREAMING:

A NEW INTERPRETIVE TOOL KIT

MICHELLA CLARK

BALBOA.PRESS
A DIVISION OF HAY HOUSE

Balboa Press books may be ordered through booksellers or by contacting:

Balboa Press
A Division of Hay House
1663 Liberty Drive
Bloomington, IN 47403
www.balboapress.com
844-682-1282

Interior image credit: Athena Lutton

Print information available on the last page.

ISBN: 979-8-7652-5126-3 (sc)
ISBN: 979-8-7652-5125-6 (e)

Library of Congress Control Number: 2024908104

Balboa Press rev. date: 08/16/2024

DEDICATION

To all the dreamers the world over who awaken in the morning and wish they knew just what that dream meant. I hope this helps.

CONTENTS

FOREWORD

I awoke to the sight of a beautiful face leaning over me. Except for her dark brown eyes, the rest of her face was covered by a mask, and her hair covered by a scarf. I wondered, absurdly, if she was a beekeeper. Why else would someone be completely covered up?

She asked me if I remembered anything, like what day or year it was. I told her I thought it was 2020. I couldn't quite remember the day or where I was—or why.

Then, it came back to me. I was in the hospital. I had been diagnosed with acute respiratory distress syndrome (ARDS) due to a severe case of COVID-19. The nurse, not a beekeeper after all, informed me I had been intubated for eight days.

The world had changed in those eight days. When I was admitted into the intensive care unit, there were no mask requirements. COVID was just a small statistic in Colorado, and I had never been seriously sick before in my life. When I was brought out of the coma, everyone I saw had personal protective equipment (PPE) on and Colorado was on lockdown.

As I was coming back into consciousness, I wondered briefly if I was incarcerated in a mental institute. I fell back to sleep, or what passed for sleep after being in a coma for more than a week. Then, in the half-light of consciousness, I had the most life-changing dream I've ever had.

I would say now, a few years later, that dream was the beginning of my new life. Having meaningful dreams was not unusual or new to me. I had been engaged in analyzing dreams for decades. But my new life started that night, in a semi-dark ICU room with lots of whirring machines and inhabited by what looked like a colony of beekeepers.

Here it is, as I wrote the dream down a few days later....

The God of Second Chances

...I woke up in a hospital room. I remembered I was in the hospital, and I recognized the room as the room in real life that I think I had been in for a day or two. I wondered if I was awake or asleep. I couldn't tell. A man was standing in the corner of the room. It was a very small room and had lots of equipment with monitors and flashing lights. The man was dressed as a doctor, but I didn't recognize him. He was of medium height and had medium-brown hair. He was nondescript overall. He looked at me and then said, "What do you want in life?"

I said, "Peace."

He nodded. "Good," he seemed to say. Or, maybe he meant, "Yes, you can have peace, if that's what you want."

Even during the dream, I didn't know why I said, "Peace."

With that, he opened a door behind him, and I looked out on a green rolling pasture with big leafy trees and a bubbling brook on the right side of a large field. The geography looked like the Midwest. All my friends and family were there. My horse was there. She was standing under the trees by the brook. My husband was also there. He was by the door, outside on the left side of the pasture. He beckoned me to come through the door and into the pasture. It was an idyllic scene. Everyone was very happy to see me. It was like a big picnic.

The doctor then said I could have anything I wanted. I just had to take a few steps.

I don't know when I actually awoke. Suddenly I realized I *was* awake, and I rubbed my eyes, certain the man would not be there. I was in the hospital room I had dreamed about, and the man *was* still there. He stood quietly waiting in the corner of the room. He smiled at me. I wasn't afraid. I knew everything was going to be all right. I wasn't going to die. I had something I was meant to do here on earth. Then, he faded from view. I rubbed my eyes even harder, trying to regain my focus. Although I have had many dreams in my life; precognitive, past life, warning and solution dreams, this is the only vision dream I have ever had. It was quietly powerful in a way I had never experienced. I felt blessed and protected by his presence and I continue to feel that presence to this day.

After a while, a nurse came into my room, and I asked if the doctor had stopped by. She told me no, that he did his rounds in the afternoon. The nurse said, "You're a miracle, you know." I later found out that not many patients survived a ventilator at that time. And, of those who did survive, very few still had a functional voice after eight days on a ventilator. The pandemic had struck, and our medical professionals had few options then to save patients who had severe cases of COVID 19.

Sometime later, I was released from the hospital and returned home. I was still very weak, on oxygen, but I knew the vision-dream would be very important to me in the future. I decided to write it down and list what I wanted since the "doctor" had told me I could have anything. Later in this book, I recount the items on that list and explain how they came about.

From then on, my intuitive abilities became much stronger, my dreams more informative, and a sense of my purpose here on this earth more focused.

So, who was that man I presumed to be the doctor? That unassuming figure has become a guardian of sorts to me. I recounted the dream to my mother-in-law a few days after I got home from the hospital. She told me I had been visited by the God of Second Chances. I liked that idea. And so I titled the dream, "The God of Second Chances."

For more than forty years, I have been recording, analyzing, and working with my dreams and those of others. I have a dream library with journals detailing thousands of dreams, and a lot of attendant real-life experience with how dreams communicate. I believe the gift of dreams exists for all of us to utilize.

I'd like to help you by pointing the way to more happiness, more prosperity, more wellness, and more of whatever is beneficial in your life's journey—through accessing the information and wisdom of your dreams. This isn't a magic formula you must divine nor a philosophical hurdle to which you must advance. The information is naturally accessible to you. It is yours by God-given right. It is yours even if you don't believe in God. Just like your breath or your sleep is a natural gift of life, so is your ability to acquire valuable insight through your dreams. Dreaming is as much a physical truth of physical life as is the necessity for sleep.

I have made the process simple, trying to avoid philosophizing and instead sharing lots of real-life examples to get you started. Every dream detailed in this book was someone's actual dream. Those dreams are related to real lives with real-life choices and real-life consequences. But how do you make those life decisions, and based on what information?

Why not use all the available tools? It's my privilege to be your copilot on this journey. I'm on board and ready to help. At the end of this book, I provide you with my website address in case your dreams require a bit more analysis. I'm happy to help.

SECTION ONE

A New Way of Understanding Your Dreams

CHAPTER ONE

TO BEGIN

Have you ever woken in the middle of the night, clapped a hand to your forehead, and asked yourself, "What could *that* dream mean?"

You probably just went back to sleep, and by morning, the dream was long forgotten—your whole day ahead of you with things to do, decisions to make, and life unfolding at top speed.

What was that dream again?

This book is about learning to use your dreams as part of your arsenal for living better day to day, making wiser decisions, and understanding your life's purpose. Using your dreams takes very little time and will surprise you with insights and solutions to your everyday dilemmas.

Dreams have always been part of my life. Dreams have always been part of yours, too. Everybody dreams, just like everybody sleeps. We don't typically question the phenomena of sleep. We take sleep for granted as a therapeutic necessity. In case you need a refresher course on how critical sleep is to your well-being, I recommend reading *Why We Sleep: Unlocking the Power of Sleep and Dreams*. Dr. Matthew Walker's book provides great excuses to take more naps. It could be the answer to world peace.

Just kidding.

Kind of.

We consciously know sleep has a purpose in our waking lives, and we are now discovering that dreams have an equally vital purpose to our

1

waking selves. You use sleep to nourish and refresh your body, and you can use dreams to nourish your soul, correct your course, bring meaning to your life, and plan your future.

The connection between sleep and dreams

Dreaming is an activity embedded in the most basic sleep behavior of all humans. About eight billion people are on this planet, and all of them sleep and all of them dream, whether the dreams are remembered or not. The purpose of sleep is not only to refresh body and mind, but also to dream.

Yes, dream.

Why does sleeping necessitate dreaming? Nature is the ultimate pragmatist. So, if dreaming weren't necessary, the ever-evolving human race would have eliminated that behavior long ago. After all, sleeping and dreaming take up an enormous amount of time that could be spent gathering food, procreating, protecting the young and participating in other life-sustaining activities.

Therefore, dreaming has a very real purpose, which involves keeping us alive and happy.

Why happy? Because happy people create. They create children, food supplies, protection, enterprises and knowledge. Happy people create systems of knowledge and networks of emotional support, which lead to the continuation of the human race—one of our prime directives.

Dreams are not just flimsy snippets of detritus left over from our daytime experiences. It is illogical to believe dreams don't mean anything, aren't accurate, or can't be useful. They are just too prevalent in the human experiences, too consistently part of our sleep, to not be a relevant and vital part of our lives.

Many civilizations have famously recorded dreams and their usefulness. The Bible, in the book of Genesis, cites a prisoner, Joseph, who was able to interpret the Egyptian pharaoh's recurring dream of seven lean cows devouring seven fat cows to predict a famine. That interpretation saved the Egyptian population from a seven-year famine and certain starvation. Joseph was amply rewarded for his dream insight. He was released from prison, pardoned, and promoted to prime minister of Egypt. Not a bad return for a bit of dream analysis.

Self-taught mathematician Srinivasa Ramanujan, in a dream on his deathbed in 1920, described mysterious mathematical functions that mimicked theta functions, or modular forms. These functions became the basis for string theory, a mathematical explanation of how the universe was created. I admit that string theory is a bit of an esoteric concept for me, but I love the idea that mathematics can explain the universe. It's comforting, somehow.

Harriet Tubman's heroic work with the Underground Railroad—rescuing slaves from the South and leading them to safety in the North—is another beautiful example of the usefulness of dreams. Harriet used her dreams to find geographical routes she had never been on before to guide her parties to safe places. It sounds improbable, and yet it happened.

These are just a few accounts of dreams that have changed nations, saved people, and increased humankind's knowledge. We are gifted as humans with this ability to dream and receive solutions to help better humanity as well as help us individually in our everyday lives.

From a practical perspective, if there is information that can be utilized toward your goals or aspirations, shouldn't you use it? We use our intuition, knowledge, prayers, meditations, priests, and shamans to guide us, so why not use this tool as well? Think of your dreams as your best friends in life. Dreams will always have your back, always seeking to provide you with valuable insight.

You will still need to take action. Dreams do not solve your problems. They advise and illuminate, but do not solve. That's your part of the equation.

What your dreams can do for you

Here's what to expect on this journey:

- Embrace the connection between sleep and dreams and know why that's important.
- Understand how your dreams are *always* on your side to help and guide you.

3

- Create your own dream symbol notebook, which is much better than a dream dictionary.
- Adopt a DIY step-by-step process for analyzing your dreams through a Dream Cypher.
- Get a heads-up for proactive problem-solving.
- Ignite your intuition for daily use.
- Make better decisions even when you don't have all the information.
- Live your best life with guidance from your inner wisdom.

Let's begin.

CHAPTER TWO

WHY DREAMS ARE IMPORTANT

Dreams are important because understanding and acting on them can transform your world and even the world at large. Dreams can provide you with knowledge that adds to your everyday thinking.

Physicist David Deutsch, in his book *The Beginning of Infinity: Explanations That Transform the World*, beautifully explains the power of knowledge: "The ability to create and use explanatory knowledge gives people a power to transform nature which is ultimately not limited by parochial factors, as all other adaptations are, but only by universal laws. This is the cosmic significance of explanatory knowledge."

In simpler words, explanatory knowledge has the power to share answers to questions and affect change by reasoned action. One source of such knowledge is the wealth of insight and wisdom acquired from dreams.

Take Paul McCartney, who dreamed the entire melody for the Beatles song "Yesterday" in one night. Upon waking, he wrote down the melody and then asked his friends if they had ever heard the song, as he was suspicious at that point of the gift of dreams. None had heard the melody before. So, he and John Lennon published "Yesterday," which became one of the most recorded songs in history. McCartney is now, understandably, a believer in the value of his dreams.

This book explains how dreams work, helping you to remember, understand, and use your dreams to transform your life. There are many paths to knowledge, but few provide everyday answers for all of your uniqueness. Everything you need to begin using your dream wisdom to transform your world is embodied in chapters that include, for example, the following:

- How to ignite your intuition and contact your inner Dream Sherpa.
- How to use your personal dream GPS, the Dream CypherTM.
- Dream examples from real people, and their meanings, to further illustrate use of the Dream Cypher tool.
- Common dream types. You will learn to recognize what kinds of dreams you are having and what to do with them. Not all dreams are created equal. Some are expressions of inner fears, others are insightful, and some are straightforward warnings.

A note about dream symbols

Dream symbols are the vocabulary of dreams. You will learn to understand your personal symbols, which you will find much more useful than the generic symbols featured in dream dictionaries. The Dream Cypher is a tool for easily decoding your dreams. By responding to key prompts and following the process, you'll understand the information your dreams provide and their connections to your daily life.

While I don't focus on the spirituality of dreams in this book, I believe a strong connection to the superconscious, or the soul, happens while dreaming. I wrote this book for those who want some practical answers to life's issues, as a complement to their spiritual understanding and their innate reason.

Become the alchemist of your life. The tools are at hand.

CHAPTER THREE

A Different Kind
of Dream Book

What kind of dream could possibly help you decide in which school to enroll your kids, who is a good partner for you, how to find a solution to your health issues, or what your business needs are in order to thrive?

I understand your reluctance to add one more thing to your "should-do" list. I intend to give you a new perspective on your dreams, not just repackage another dream dictionary with the same dream symbols that have been around for years—new thinking, not new clothes.

My problem with dream dictionaries or other methods for labeling dreams is that genuine dream symbols have innate meanings that are specific to you and bundled into the context of a story by your dreaming self. You can mine this wisdom only through self-reflection. Whatever the label is for your dream, be it "lucid," the kind of a dream where you are aware that you are dreaming or "incubator," the kind of dream where you dream of a solution to a problem that you have in your waking life, how it helps you is, in the end, is all that matters.

There's a process to gaining practical guidance from your dreams. Analyzing and using your dreams require an organized process even a librarian could love. I have a not-so-secret librarian as an alter ego. To assuage that part of my brain, I insert dreams of my own or others in italicized text so I—and my librarian proclivities—can better articulate how to put this process into action. You will be able to easily discern the dream material, which is set in italics, from the main narrative content.

Below is an example of a dream with a subsequent NB notation to describe what was happening to me at the time. NB is the abbreviation for *nota bene*, which in Latin means "note well" or "pay attention." I use it to make personal comments about my dreams' connections with insights into my waking life.

Calculator Necklace

...I had a calculator around my neck, wearing it as a necklace. It was cumbersome, awkward, and not that pretty.

NB: I was pregnant at the time. I was busily counting up all the money we spent, budgeting every penny and fretting over each minor infraction of the budget—probably not an attractive trait for a newlywed.

Could that dream have been useful? Yes, I could have stopped with the nagging and enjoyed those first days of being a wife and a mother. Did I?

No. Note to self: Knowing and doing are two very different things.

I assure you dreams can help with those types of decisions as well as many other more esoteric questions. I will show you how to analyze your dreams for practical advice on just about any subject.

So, why not a dream dictionary?

Why this book, and not a dream dictionary? Because learning to decipher your dreams by using dream symbols from a dream dictionary is like using a coloring book to learn to paint your masterpiece. A dream dictionary reduces symbols to the lowest common denominator. How to understand your dreams comes from understanding your own personal symbols in all of their complexity within the context of those symbols. Don't be reductive.

Meet your Dream Sherpa

Take the phrase "man bites dog." Knowing what a man is and what a dog is and what a bite is doesn't really help to understand what the sentence is communicating.

Are you with me?

Knowing that the man bit the dog is a clear statement of an action. But that's not all the statement is communicating. The author of that statement is saying this is surprising and an unexpected, turn of events that is not normal. We understand that interpretation because of the context of those words, not because we understand the words.

Let's say you dream of a snake. A snake symbol can mean a "snake in the grass," in reference to a person who is not what he or she seems to be on the surface. That explanation might come up as a dream dictionary definition. Or the snake can refer to a hidden circumstance that will reveal itself to be dangerous. Or it can mean ancient wisdom, as in Egyptian mythology in which the cobra symbolized Wadjet—the goddess who was believed by ancient Egyptians to help prevent chaos and preserve peace.

If you haven't analyzed the plot of a dream along with its symbols or people within the dream—nor factored in your personal opinion of snakes—it's not helpful to know that the symbol of a snake means either betrayal, danger ahead, or wisdom about preserving peace. What are you supposed to do about betrayal or danger if you don't know where it is coming from? And how does believing a snake represents wisdom lead you to apply that wisdom in your life?

Some symbols are useful for gaining a general idea of what the dream is communicating. For example, a car usually refers to one's way of moving through life or a particular path through life. However, what kind of car it is, what color it is and who is driving the car are the important features of the symbols.

Reading in a dream dictionary about a symbol's possible meaning without context does not necessarily lead to a conversation with your inner wisdom. And that's the real goal—to understand what your inner wisdom, your Dream Sherpa, is communicating to you. Your particular symbol language is both a shared language because of the culture you have been raised in and a unique language colored by your singular experiences. Your job is to make use of your dream sherpa so you can train your dreams to provide you with useful information. This book will provide templates to guide you to that understanding.

Why your personal dream symbols are important to understand

Famed psychoanalyst Carl Jung's *Man and His Symbols* is an excellent book for understanding the deeper nature of dreams and symbols across a civilization. But that doesn't necessarily help with everyday issues. What if you need some idea of how to pay your bills that doesn't include felonious endeavors, or how to raise your kids without marooning them for twenty years on an island with a patient nanny, or maybe how to keep from locking up your boss in a padded (but comfy) cell?

These are the problems dreams love to solve. Dreams exist to help you survive and thrive. At the most basic level of human programming, we are here to be happy and healthy, and to continue to evolve humankind.

Over the years, I have trained my dreams to communicate with me in such a way that I can understand my options for navigating through my life. I use my dreams to gather answers to everyday practical questions, to understand more esoteric questions, and to even get answers about how to save my business from bankruptcy.

A book of dream symbols can get you thinking in the right direction about how dreams communicate to you, but first you must understand your personal symbols and your own reality in the context of a dream story.

Igniting your intuition

Understanding your dream symbols—and the stories that illuminate your dreams—ignites your intuition and provides you with insight into your very special life potential. That, in turn, transforms your current life.

In fact, information on just about anything you want an answer for can come through your dreams. You can then develop an action plan through your newly inspired intuition.

The practical applications of dreams

If you are expecting me to tell you that you must meditate, go vegan, or hop on the next flight to Tibet...well, not quite. While I like those ideas in theory, I will stick to the practical, what-you-can-do-today suggestions. I'm all about practical applications.

If you just want to kick your life up a step, and not become a monk or change up your Friday night pizza date, then help is here. Small steps to integrate your dreams into your waking life can have huge repercussions throughout your lifetime. I know this for a fact, and I give you real-life examples of dream solutions to difficult problems, such as finding a lost child, avoiding bankruptcy, and dealing with drug problems—some of the more dramatic dream solutions. Insight into relationships, business opportunities, or bringing more fun into your life are also possible.

Meditation helps

While meditation is not required, I highly recommend it. I find meditation brings calm to my everyday life, usually allowing more solutions to flow to my consciousness. There are several methodologies to choose from, and I leave that entirely up to you. The templates that I provide to help with dream analysis are in the appendix.

Every life has challenges

I want answers to my life's challenges, and I've used my dreams to help me to find access to those answers. You, too, can access answers from your dreams, ignite your intuition for everyday use, and learn to trust your gut.

In the next few chapters, I take you through an overview of the various kinds of dreams. You'll find a step-by-step process to heighten your ability to use dreams and intuition for guidance. This will help you choose daily actions that are in line with what you want out of your life.

So, find a notebook, your soon-to-be Dream Workbook. If you prefer to dictate into your iPhone or write dreams down in your iPad, that's fine, too. The important thing is to set aside about ten minutes each morning to develop the habit of detailing your dreams.

Everything you need to know

Everything you need to know to get started is in the following chapters. Here's an overview:

- A detailed list of steps to take, as well as examples of dreams analyzed by using the Dream Cypher.
- How to remember and record your dreams.
- Explanations of the different types of dreams.
- How to create your unique symbol dictionary.
- Using your dreams as your personal board of directors to manifest your best life.
- Using your dreams to increase your intuitive abilities during the day.
- A small dictionary of common symbols to the American culture, just to get you thinking about your own symbols.

In short, in the following pages you will find a map and all the tools needed for this journey—except for the hiking boots.

SECTION TWO

Your New Tool Kit

CHAPTER ONE

PRACTICAL TOOLS FOR
USEFUL DREAMING

I began to take my dreams seriously at about age nineteen, but I was quite young, about twelve, when I developed the practice of writing down my dreams. I didn't immediately make strong connections between my written dreams and my reality. I had read many books on dreams by authors such as Carl Jung and clairvoyant Edgar Cayce, who claimed to absorb the contents of books by keeping them under his pillow while he slept. I decided to do the same, and I placed Cayce's *Dreams and Visions* under my pillow to more fully understand my dreams.

Easy, right? That night, I had this dream:

Cream Pies and Volleyballs

> *...I was playing volleyball but, instead of a ball, I was playing with cream pies. Every time I threw a cream pie, it splattered in someone's face.*

Everyone's a comic—even my dreams. I was being told I didn't yet have the equipment to use my dreams. It was unlikely I would hurt someone, but the exercise was comical in its implications. Maybe this wasn't going to be as easy as I thought.

I resolved to learn more and get better at dream interpretation. I kept up with my dream notebooks, reading about dreams, and asking more questions. My advice is to just take the first step. Write down or otherwise record your dreams. The rest will follow.

How dreams work

Our dreams use symbols to bundle up meanings. That's how dreams work—they tell stories. Dreams use the symbols that have meaning to you. At first, these symbols may seem obscure or even silly. But that is the beauty of working with your dream symbols. Later in this book, I provide templates to record your dreams and their symbols, so you can track the symbols that crop up frequently in your dreams.

The purpose of dream symbols is to help you know your psyche and tap into your wisdom. Most of us fail to rely on the inner wisdom we all have inherently. Your inner wisdom has a purpose and a personality. Yes, I really mean personality. You might believe dreams come from spirit guides, divine spirit, God, or some other higher power, but your body and mind know things you don't fully give them credit for. Your intuition communicates with you all the time. Most of the time, people don't listen.

Dreams come more easily when you are in a particularly relaxed and receptive state. Brain experts say sleep heals the brain from trauma and depression. I believe this applies to healthy dream states as well. Dr. Sanjay Gupta's book *Keep Sharp: Build a Better Brain at Any Age* details the process of keeping your brain fit for your whole life. In the process of washing out all the bad receptors and rebuilding good ones, your brain also receives information in the form of dreams.

Dream information comes in the form of a story filled with symbols and emotion—and sometimes an admonishment if you are not behaving in ways that support your best interests.

How to use this book

I've divided this book into sections. The first is about why dreams are important to you and how to begin interpreting them. It explains the tools you will need and what you will learn.

The second section addresses the process for making your dreams useful. The chapter titled "Introducing the Dream Cypher Template" details the exact process for recording your dreams. After learning this, you will have the basics down for understanding your dreams.

The third section helps you create order from pieces of a dream to make the appropriate connections to your waking life. It also illustrates the process by showcasing real dreams from real people.

The chapter titled "Understanding Common Dream Types" explains the various categories of dreams, so you can understand what kind of dream you had and what to expect from that dream in terms of insight.

The final section elucidates the interactive role of intuition and action with the information derived from dreams.

First, you must make some preparations, which I address here in order of importance:

Commit to recording your dreams.

You will need to write down or otherwise record your dreams over time to gain the best guidance available. If you don't remember your dreams, get into the habit of jotting down how you feel upon waking from slumber. I recommend not moving for a few minutes in the morning upon waking. If you prefer not to journal, use your cell phone to record your dreams. If you remember only a few snippets of a dream, tell the story, to yourself, in as much detail as possible. Give it a title. Later, if you recall the title, it usually brings to mind the rest of the dream. The most important factor is to record the dream, no matter how you get that done.

Choose your notebook or another method for recording your dreams.

This is essential because you need one place to keep track of your dream information. I refer to this as a Dream Workbook. Begin to note the symbols your dreams use to get your attention or to show you deeper aspects of the symbol's meaning. I provide templates for each type of dream, to organize your dream information and make it easier to see recurring patterns.

As I matured, married, and had kids, I maintained my habit of writing down my dreams. I first wrote them in a notebook, but then couldn't find the ones I wanted to analyze. So, I decided on a discipline I've used for many years. I fill a five-inch-by-nine-inch unlined, hardbound book with dreams until I finish the last page. Then, I label the spine of the book beginning with the date of the first dream recorded and the ending date of the last dream. I gave the dreams titles because the titles prompted me to remember whether I wanted to further analyze them.

Lately, I use a larger notebook because I like to draw the imagery that comes to me in dreams. In this case, I type my dreams on an iPad, and then print out and paste the words next to the image I've drawn. But you choose whatever works for you.

Choose a format that differentiates dream data from your comments about the dream.

I always start with an ellipsis (three little dots that look like this: "…") to indicate the content is dream material, not real-life events or my thoughts. This technique came to me when I wrote in my first dream book, and I have kept it up. I write my dreams in longhand as opposed to typed or dictated, except as noted above. I find this works best for me. I intermingle real-life events that I believe pertain to the subject of the dream, along with dream material, as I want to distinguish between my recorded dream and my written commentary about that dream. Each dream starts with an ellipsis, and my comments about the dream are introduced with "NB", meaning Note Bene, or note well.

In the Basic Dream Cypher Template, I also write down snippets of songs that come to me upon waking. These usually set a tone for the day. Later in the book, I share more about my spiritual DJ. Song snippets can help you quickly identify the day's issues. Use whatever clarifying format works for you.

Somehow, the connection between pen and paper makes the notating process flow for me. I keep my favorite pen and my Dream Workbook beside my bed. It is best to write down your dreams right away. Don't get up and start your day before writing down the dream, because you might forget its context or a scrap of an image that could be crucial to the dream's information.

Apply the use of "NB."

As mentioned, I write "NB" at the beginning of the paragraph after the recorded dream to remind me to pay attention to certain elements related to my interpretation of the dream. I put that symbol in after writing down my dreams, to integrate my daily thoughts with the dream symbols. The NB inspires me to look for connections I might have missed because of the natural separation we tend to apply in reacting to real-life events and observing dream-life events.

It helps me understand why certain symbols crop up in my dreams and how they correspond to my everyday life. It gives me perspective on my life's happenings that need clarification. If these sound like illogical leaps, that is the way dreams work—one pebble at a time that only you will recognize. Once you put down these images and make the everyday life connections to the imagery, you will discover the guidebook to your symbols.

After writing down my dream, I spend a little time thinking about feelings the dream brings up. Or maybe it brings to mind an event that reminds me of, or is connected to, the dream's events. I don't start these thoughts with an ellipsis, like I do for dreams. I write them down following NB, which signals to me that this is a waking life commentary.

Use the Dream Cypher templates.

I have developed a series of templates to help unravel your dreams and illuminate your personal symbols. It is modified for distinct types of dreams, and step-by-step instructions are provided in each section featured in the chapter titled "Understanding Common Dream Types."

Don't edit or judge your dreams while recording them.

This bears repeating. I will remind you several times not to edit or judge your dreams while you are writing them down. The single most important factor when recording your dreams is to not think about them at all except to record them. Before finishing the recording of the dream, you might lose the context of the message by prejudging the appropriateness of its imagery. That will influence your perceptions and, therefore, the recordings of your dreams. While you are learning to understand your personal symbols, give yourself the leeway to mix metaphors, intertwine your stories, and draw from whatever symbols you would like to use—not just the metaphors, stories, or symbols you find to be acceptable in your waking life. This broadens your dream vocabulary to put you in touch with how you really view your life's issues.

Write it down exactly as it comes to you.

Right about now, you might be saying, "I don't remember my dreams, and my mornings are crazy busy. No way am I getting into the lotus position and smiling while I write down what seems to me like a silly story."

Okay, fair enough. Still, take a few minutes to jot down your dream, or grab your cell phone and dictate it into the phone. You can look at it later. The main objective is to record the events without the editing your conscious mind does.

Also, if you remember an incident, don't try to decide whether it was part of a dream or not part of a dream. Just write it down. With the habit of consistently writing down your dreams (or voice-recording them), you'll start to figure out what your inner wisdom is trying to tell you.

Be truthful and ignore your inner editor.

I like to write down my dreams because I feel the process of writing precludes activating the inner editor of the spoken word. Most of us have been taught not to say everything we think. For example, take that inner editor that kicks in when you see in a dream your favorite nephew sticking needles into his sister. It works like this: You start to record your dream or tell it to someone. "Ahem," you say, "Maddie was sticking pins in—"

"No," your inner editor says, "Maddox would never do that to his sister."

So, you write down instead, "Maddox seemed a little irritated at his sister." This is not necessarily helpful information for you, as you are absolving Maddox of causing pain and not acknowledging your dream about that pain. Maybe you have witnessed Maddox making caustic comments to his sister. Sort of okay, you think. Kids will be kids. But, if Maddox is so mean-spirited to his sister that, when you dream, you see his comments as physically sticking pins into his sister, that is not okay.

Or maybe dream-state Maddox represents someone who is a bit caustic toward you. You are not recognizing the stabs of pain, which the pins symbolize. Or perhaps you have been mean-spirited toward your sibling, and this dream is a wake-up call to change your behavior.

When you dream, you remember things your conscious mind edits out when you speak—at least most of us don't say everything we think. (Looking at you, Mom!) Keep that editor at bay so you fully understand the message. If you are verbally recording your dreams, beware the editor!

Make connections between your dream images and your waking life observations.

Whatever connections come into your mind, write them down as well. It could be a phrase someone said to you, a recent observation, or a snippet of a song that comes to mind. Pay attention to the clues that float into your awareness.

Something else that will help you understand the clues to your dream messages is to notice any imagery or coincidences previewed in your dreams that appear in your life. Sometimes it is an image, a song, or a person.

Years ago, the refrain of "Raindrops Keep Fallin' on My Head" came into my mind upon awakening. At first, I just thought I had recently heard the song, so it was stuck in my brain. Then I realized I hadn't heard that song in years. In fact, I couldn't remember most of the words.

I was in the middle of the worst financial crisis of my life, as many of us were during the Great Recession of 2008. It seemed every day brought a new disaster. The lyrics of the song are about not letting 'the rain' depress your spirit.

From that point on, I paid attention to what I termed my "spiritual DJ" to concisely convey a tidbit of perspective on my emotional well-being. The abovementioned song was telling me I wouldn't always be under pressure and that the blues wouldn't defeat me. Happiness was right around the corner.

Pay attention to the songs whispering to you. This helps when you just need some quick insight. Also notice the sticky images in your life—they are there for a purpose. What I mean by "sticky images" is when you find yourself noticing something with particular focus. Or you make a connection between what someone said to you and what you are now experiencing.

Other waking symbols to reinforce your dream material can be anything—an unexpected call from someone, a book title or quote, or witnessing something that makes a "sticky" impression on you. A waking symbol that reinforced my spiritual DJ's song about raindrops came in the form of the numbers 444.

My friend Lisa and I met for lunch one day. After I recounted some of my frustration in finding the right kind of work to relieve my financial pressure, Lisa mentioned that the numbers 444 indicated angels were listening to my entreaties. I didn't know about the angels listening, but I knew I was barely listening to my intuition. Angel numbers had never been of particular interest to me, but I liked the thought that more help was available. I awoke that night and began reading a book on my iPad— something I often do when I worry. I looked at the time, and it was 4:44 a.m. *Of course.*

I then began to see those numbers on license plates, addresses, and even receipts. I previously had no particular affinity for this number. I wasn't even attuned to angel numbers. I thought perhaps a confirmation bias was invading my space—that I was subconsciously looking for those numbers. Maybe I just wanted to feel angel numbers worked. I put my thoughts about angel numbers aside. And then this happened....

The man who mowed my lawn every other week, knocked on my studio door and held out a tiny angel figurine. "This yours?" he asked.

"No. I don't think so. I've never seen that before." But really? An angel? Delivered right to my door? "But now that you mention it, maybe so," I said. "Maybe so."

How did he find some little angel figurine that was about one inch long, tops, while mowing a big lawn? I'll never know. My lawn had been mowed every other week during spring and summer for years. No angels appeared then. But he found an angel figurine that day, and he delivered it to me. I keep that little angel on my desk to remind me not to discount the signs.

Within a short while, all my fears about what to do, who to call, and when it would happen were resolved through an opportunity that floated in as if it had been part of a script I was just now getting. Everything worked out.

Here's another example: One evening I was dining outside on the patio of a restaurant. A man walked by with a baby in his arms. I don't know why, but I watched him with great interest. I was fascinated by the way he carried that baby. I had the following dream that night.

Very Pregnant

...I was carrying a baby. I was a pregnant mother. I was very
pregnant and was going to give birth to a twelve-pound baby.

NB: Upon waking, I remembered that man carrying his baby. I thought about what it meant to carry a baby, and I wondered what a twelve-pound baby meant to me. That's an exceptionally big baby, and I realized I was being alerted to a big event coming about in my life. A dream of mine was about to come to fruition. I was going to get "pregnant" and have a "baby" bigger than expected. The number twelve in the dream might represent a very big project, or it could indicate the twelfth month for the birth of my project. I started this book in December of that year, just like my dream indicated.

CHAPTER TWO

PUTTING YOUR TOOLS TO WORK

Do you remember the sign that Plato had posted above the door to his Academy in ancient Athens? 'Let no one ignorant of geometry enter here?' Plato had a point. He was referring to the necessity of immersing oneself into geometry to invite thought and reflection, and hence enable the mind to reach truth. Secondarily, Plato thought the advanced parts of arithmetic and geometry had the power to draw the soul from *becoming* into *being*.

And you thought geometry was boring.

As a liberal extension to that philosophy, immersion into the basic effort of writing down a dream brings about understanding of your dream language, and your inner Dream Sherpa, as it relates to your day-to-day reality—your truth, in your own symbols. My perspective as it relates to dreams is that you must understand the basics of dream language, your own symbols, before you can usefully apply the knowledge of dreams. I might rewrite Plato's statement this way: "Let no one ignorant of their own dream symbols enter here."

Remembering your dreams

Here's a tip on how to remember your dreams. First, right before going to bed, tell yourself you will remember your dreams. You may have to do this for a few nights but be patient. If you wake up in the night, clearly remembering a dream, tell yourself the story of the dream—aloud, if possible. If not, just silently recount the story as if you were telling it to a child. Give the dream a title that makes sense to you—not necessarily pithy or even evocative, but illustrative. Then, go back to sleep. In the morning, ask yourself what the title was of the story you recounted in the night. Usually, the story of the dream will easily float back into your mind once it's given a title.

What if you are having nightmares and don't want to remember those?

I admit this is a dilemma. However, I still say write them down in your Dream Workbook. Analyze the dream, using the Dream Cypher template. One of the best ways to get rid of nightmares is to understand the message so you can do something about any related circumstances. Certain drugs interfere with dreams as well. If you take supplements or prescriptions to aid your sleep, these can cause disturbances in your dreams.

Nightmares that are not caused by alcohol or drugs are designed to guide you. Conquer your fear and try to understand the message. Lots of circumstances are preventable, given deeper understanding and a willingness to change. Here's an example of a nightmarish, warning dream:

Death on the Highway

> ...*My dog, Sadie, ran into the road and was hit by an eighteen-wheeler. She was killed immediately. I was frightened to even go see her body because I felt I hadn't taken good enough care of her. I was devastated and horrified that I had let this happen.*

I had this dream several nights in a row. I was afraid for my dog but didn't see how such a scenario could even happen. I didn't live near a highway, and no trucks could possibly drive fast down my narrow and winding road. Also, Sadie was never out without me, surely, I wouldn't let this happen.

Once I got past my horror and sorrow, I thought deeply about why this dream had come to me. I have a fear that my pets might be killed on the street, and I thought about what Sadie meant to me. She has always had an indomitable spirit—maybe a little too indomitable, in that she would stubbornly persist in walking down a road whether I wanted to or not.

I realized maybe I was too headstrong in my life, just like Sadie can be. I was being particularly headstrong in a specific situation, and the dream was warning me it could lead to disaster. And it did. A Foundation very dear to me had become quite toxic. I resigned from the board due to pressure from some of its other members. So, my nightmare had come true. It was the death of my relationship with that foundation, which I had begun with its founder and helped build over the course of nineteen years. I should have taken better care of my indomitable spirit and perhaps been less persistent in my direction—or at least watched out for potential collisions.

Although, I was horrified, the dream was useful to me, given the right perspective. In the next couple of chapters, specifics of the Dream Cypher template are explained in detail.

CHAPTER THREE

Introducing Your Basic Dream Cypher Template

Telling the truth in your dreams is risk-free. No judgment avatar is waiting behind the curtain. Is there really a payoff, you ask? Not every dream is worth all this effort, right? Right.

Some dreams are just clearinghouses for leftover emotions. The next chapter explains how to tell what kind of dream you are having, so you can focus your energy on those that matter. I also provide examples for quickly moving to the significant parts of a dream. Do I hear sighs of relief from the young mothers out there? This is fun and not all that time-consuming, I promise. I recommend looking for the strongest feeling-tone of a dream and choosing that dream to analyze.

Don't be afraid to tell the truth. Let the words flow out of your mind and onto the page. Let the story unfold as if you were watching a stage play. You will be incredibly surprised at how connected your intuition is to your everyday life.

How to use the Dream Cypher template

Jot down your notes on the template, available in the appendix of this book, which you can paste in your journal along with the handwritten or typed dreams you recorded. I find it is easier to make connections between your waking life and your dreaming life if you can draw images, paste quotes, or make random observations without disturbing the actual dream recollection. In the next chapter, how to use the basic Dream Cypher template is explained by way of a real-life dream analyzed with step-by-step instructions.

What follows is an outline that details the template, with explanations for how to best fill in each portion of the Dream Cypher. For this section, it is helpful to have your selected journal handy—your Dream Workbook—along with a printout of the Dream Cypher template. This template has several variations, but below is the basic outline.

BASIC DREAM CYPHER TEMPLATE

Write down the dream exactly as you remember it:

As I've said, don't edit, judge, or try to make the dream logical. Just write or record without overthinking. Try not to wait too long after you wake up. If you're awake and the dream has faded, give it a minute before getting out of bed. Recall that if you woke in the night and told yourself a story, then being still before jumping up usually brings the dream back into your consciousness. If you have a question, you want answered, add that to the "reality check" portion toward the end of the Dream Cypher template.

Tell the story of your dream by asking questions about the details of the symbols that were not in your first written version of the dream:

I refer to this as the story line of the dream. Write down the story of the dream, just as if you were storytelling. Employ the phrase, "and then what happened?" to see what other details you might notice when telling the story but didn't write down. The reason I provide a section for the story line that's separate from the original written account is that when people tell the story of their dreams aloud, almost everyone adds more insight into their dream by providing some details that were left out in the initial writing. That's the difference between recounting and storytelling.

Take note of action, direction, location, and timing:

Where did this dream take place, at what time of day, or during which season? What physical markers in the dream did you recognize—schools, streets, former houses, clothing? Were you the same age as you are now? Sometimes a past life crops up, past life here referring to a preincarnate era, usually related to an event in your current life. In those instances, you might not recognize the clothing or places—but those physical attributes should still catch your attention. What happened in the dream? What direction were you headed? Can you tell if you were going upstairs, downstairs, south, or north? What actions did you or someone else take? Was the action beneficial or harmful to you and others in your dream? These are just a few of the questions you could ask.

Describe the feeling-tone, and ignite your intuition:

How did you feel throughout the dream? How did others feel around you? What was the general emotional atmosphere of the dream? Make note of any images or feelings that rise up when you begin to analyze this dream. Images or feelings are tipoffs to how this dream is related to your waking life. Some images will become symbols for you. How do you know what is an image and what is a symbol? Ask yourself if the image you have noted arouses any particular reaction from you. For example, if your Uncle Jack appears in a dream, ask yourself what your Uncle Jack means to you. Is he your favorite Uncle? If you don't have any special feelings about him at all, then maybe he is a character in your dream but not a symbol. Here's another example, in your dream your favorite car from when you just learned how to drive appears in the driveway of the house you live in now. You loved that car! And there it is, in the driveway of your current house. Very likely that car is a symbol to you. You have strong feelings about it. Now ask yourself, 'what did that car mean to me? Freedom? Fun? Did I look good in it? Did I feel special driving it around? Was I the happiest I've ever been driving that car? Let your intuition add to your picture of what the dream is telling you. As you record your dream, add those connections into your narrative under the NB section. You will be surprised how much your personal symbols communicate.

List the symbols observed in your dream:

Symbols are the nouns of dreams. They are usually recognizable places, people, or things from this lifetime, your current circumstances, a former time in your life, or even a preincarnate past life. It could be your dog, car, or childhood home—things that mean something to you. Dream symbols use images to deliver packets of information. Which dream images got your attention?

Make note of current and relevant life events:

Write down a brief statement about anything happening in your life that might pertain to the dream. This is not always obvious, and sometimes the dream is meant to promote your growth in areas that are not on your radar right now.

Take a moment for a reality check:

What parts of your dream have a connection to your real life, whether a past, current, or future situation (such as an upcoming event like a vacation or wedding)? Did you request an answer to a question or problem, or seek any other specific information from your dreaming self? If so, add that here to the Dream Cypher.

Write a brief conclusion:

A conclusion leads to action. Confusion or ambiguity leads to inaction. Be decisive. Or take the first step to being decisive by asking more detailed questions to find out more information.

Now make an action plan:

What might you do to improve your situation, or someone else's? How can you use the information from your dream to improve your life, or others' lives?

Give your dream a title and a date:

Summarize the dream in a few words that make its main point obvious to you. Use these words as your title. This focuses your attention on the primary intent of the dream, much like a title to a book. If you have awakened in the night and are not going to write it down immediately, then tell yourself the story of the dream and give it a title. When you awaken fully, recalling the title will help you remember the details of the dream.

The next chapter provides an example of how to use the Dream Cypher template as described previously. Just print out the template and follow its prompts. As you work through the template, you will likely remember more about the dream as you retell its story line—details that didn't make it into the original written dream portion.

Let's say you remember that the house in your dream had turquoise curtains like in your aunt's house. So, in the storytelling portion of the template, you write down that forgotten detail. Or, what if your black-and-white dog was a collie in the dream instead of a boxer? Write that down. These tiny details are vital to understanding your dream symbols. If you're not sure you correctly recall the details, write them down anyway. Those scraps of memory are relevant, leading to better recall and deeper understanding of your dreams over time.

Remember to not judge or edit your writings or recordings. You are learning to listen to your intuition about your dreams, and that takes asking your inner critic to step aside for a few minutes. Follow the energy, as the Buddhists say.

CHAPTER FOUR

BASIC DREAM CYPHER TEMPLATE EXAMPLE

While dreams often seem wacky and weird, the Basic Dream Cypher is designed to help you make sense of what might initially come off as nonsensical. I provide in this book different templates for various types of dream, so first decide which kind of dream you had, and then choose the appropriate template. If you don't really know, or the dream seems to fit into several categories of dreams, use this basic template, which also appears in the back of this book for photocopying. Prompts that don't seem to further your understanding of the dream or are inapplicable will lead you to the proper template.

Effectively using the Dream Cypher template

The following is a practical example of how to use the Basic Dream Cypher template printout.

Don't Tarry

> *...Liz walked into the room where I was sitting, and she had the strong intuition to tell me to "not tarry" and list my house for sale right away.*

Write down the dream in your Dream Workbook exactly as you remember it:

See the dream titled *Don't Tarry*.

Tell the story of your dream to yourself. Then note all the details that were not in your first written version of the dream:

Liz was trying to tell me something important in my dream, so she walked back into the room I was in and told me to list the house right away. She used the words, "don't tarry." She wasn't worried but was just emphasizing what needed to be done. I think we were at my house.

Take note of action, direction, location, and timing:

The action in the dream was direct. Liz was emphatic about selling the house right away. The timing was right now. I think the location was our current house.

List the symbols observed in your dream:

There was only Liz telling me to get on with it—no real symbols.

Make note of current and relevant life events:

I was getting the house ready to sell at the time of this dream. I hadn't actually listed it yet.

Take a moment for a reality check:

Yes, I could see that the market was particularly good for selling the house. I thought the market would hold for a while.

Write a brief conclusion:

I decided I should list right away, if possible.

Now make an action plan:

I chose to continue painting and getting the house ready to sell. It would take a month or so, but I thought that was a good plan.

Give your dream a title:

Don't Tarry is this dream's title.

NB: It took me a month to get my house ready to list. When interest rates went up without warning, the real estate market dropped very quickly. Consequently, the house didn't sell as I had planned. I shouldn't have tarried. I had been warned.

CHAPTER FIVE

DREAM SYMBOL NOTEBOOK
FOR THE DREAM-SERIOUS

Me, to my middle daughter: "Just try it. Write down whatever comes into your mind about your dream when you first wake up. Don't get coffee. Don't move around. Just write. Oh, and remember to take note of the symbols."

Middle daughter: "Let me get this straight. You mean, first thing in the morning I get up, no coffee. No moving around. I write everything down I can remember about a scrap of a dream while fending off the kids who are so hungry, they are trying to eat the cat. Oh, and I need to remember to take note of the symbols as well?"

Yeah, I get that a lot. Unless you have an inkling of understanding how your dreams and your dream symbols can help you, why would anyone spend the time to do it? There is a wonderful quote by Patti Smith, the musician, that advises us to hold fast to those people, ideas, and books that magnify our spirits. Dream symbols will help you realize what a wealth of knowledge you have from your sleeping life. I suggest underlining any symbols that strike you as interesting when you write down your dreams. That way, you can keep track of them and take note of when they come up again. The symbols are packets of insight for your use in your waking life. Here's an example of a particularly interesting symbol from one of my dreams.

Wadjet

> *...I sat up in bed and saw a large king cobra hovering over me at the end of the bed. It was at least ten feet high and as big around as a person's body. It was swaying to and fro, not threatening me but hovering over me. I wasn't afraid. I waved my hand to shoo the large snake away. It glided away soundlessly. I felt it was there to protect me.*

Insight from your personal dream symbols

Symbols are crucial because they consolidate insight for you into profound imagery. This imagery has layers of meaning for you specifically. In the case of the dream above, a snake the size of the one in my dream would usually elicit fear on my part, but because it didn't, I went further to intuitively connect that large king cobra image with something of relevance to me. I love ancient Egyptian symbols and when I began investigating cobras, I came across the story of Wadjet, a goddess of ancient Egypt whose personal symbol was a king cobra. I realized that I was being shown a symbol of protection and possibly, my need for it. This section is dedicated to figuring out your personal symbols. Lots of dream dictionaries purportedly explain what an image means in a dream. These serve a purpose in getting you to think about the symbols that crop up in your dreams. However, some images you will receive are unique to you. For example, my Uncle Jack isn't going to show up in a dream dictionary, but he has shown up in my dreams. Several times.

Because dream dictionaries feature generic content, they cannot interpret your personal symbols. Use the Dream Cypher template to note your dream symbols. That way you can keep track of them while analyzing your dreams. Pay particular attention to characters, animals, and locations that occur frequently across your dreams. Then, by using the template when they appear, you have a record of the circumstances and meanings around those symbols. After a while, you will understand what your personal symbols represent and how those symbols relate to what is happening in your life.

The sample symbol worksheet keeps your personal symbols very visible to you. However, it is a bit of work at first. The sample worksheet below lists some common dream symbols. I suggest that you copy the basic symbols below and ask yourself if any of those symbols appear in your dreams. Then, ask yourself if the questions listed after the symbol clarify what that dream symbol means to you. For instance, if you are driving a car, what kind of car is it? What kind of road are you on? If the car is red, small and flashy but not being driven by you, are you being 'taken for a ride?' by a flashy but insincere person? If any other images come up, make a note of them.

How do you know what a symbol is? Good question. You will get a feel for it after writing your dreams down for a little while. Is a tree always a symbol? No. But, maybe for you it is, particularly if it appears often in your dreams. Your intuition will help you as you go along. Have faith.

All symbols in your dreams are adding to the storyline and the storyline will aid in your understanding of what the dream is communicating. When it comes to dream symbols, context is everything. Ask yourself if any of these descriptors are pertinent to your dream. Make a note of the connection.

Dream Symbol Worksheet

Horses: Depending on what kind of horse, and what the horse is doing, the meanings are quite different.

- **What kind of horse?** Racehorse, work horse, retired horse, baby horse?
- **Characteristics of the horse?** Large, small, nice, threatening?

For example: Bud, my palomino paint, is a draft horse. Draft horses are bred to pull carts and wagons—a work horse rather than a racehorse. Bud symbolizes my workplace and work energy, and how I'm operating within it. If, in a dream, he is trying to squeeze under a barn door to eat but is too heavy to get under the door, then all is not well with my workplace.

Or, if a draft horse can't get back in the barn and is trying to squeeze under the door, that is an image of an unproductive workplace (barn) with a too-heavy workforce (overweight draft horse).

My mare, Miss Dublin, an Irish-bred sport horse, is indicative of my spirit and my spiritual energy level. So, if I dream, she is jumping over cars, scaling walls, or otherwise behaving as a magnificent horse, then all is well with my spirit. If she is lethargically lying down in a field and refusing to eat, my spiritual energy is low.

Houses: If you dream of a house, pay attention to where it is located or from what period the house dates. Also, what part of the house are you in? What is happening to the house?

- *Attics:* This usually refers to a spiritual perspective, sometimes related to your spiritual life.
- *Basements:* What is in the basement of your thoughts—your subconscious? What are you afraid of or ashamed of?
- *Downstairs:* Practical issues are represented by the entry level of your house. What are the issues you have at hand? What day-to-day issue needs examining?
- *Upstairs:* Where are your aspirations taking you? Is there spiritual advice in the message?

Vehicles of any kind

- *Cars:* If it's your car and you're driving, this symbol often refers to your path in life and how well you are navigating that path. If it's someone else's car, who is driving, where are they going, and are you a passenger—willing or unwilling?
- Boats? Are you on the water, on a dock, sinking or sailing?
- Bicycles? Is it easy or hard to ride?
- Trains? Do you know where you are going?

Roads: This is usually a life path reference. Is it a bumpy, long, or steep road? Pay close attention to the surrounding areas, and the time of day or night. What about the road—do you like or dislike it?

- Rough?
- Smooth?
- Highway?
- Unused road?
- Easy to follow?
- Dangerous?

Jewelry: This typically represents spiritual or material gifts, usually a sign of progress. If you are stealing jewelry in the dream, you are assuming benefit of the gift without working for it. If you are adorned with jewelry, you are being rewarded for living well.

Angels or other spiritual beings: These are rare. However, if you are visited by someone recognizable or not, pay attention to the advice given to you. You have been selected for something special. Sometimes these visions appear to remind you that you are protected or chosen for a task.

Water: If the water is deep and surrounding your house, this is potentially a warning about your financial security being under water, so to speak. If you are crossing water in the dream, take note of how you are making the journey and where you are going.

Eggs: Eggs symbolize creations, whether your own or someone else's. What are you bringing forth, or what is someone else producing?

Snakes: Snakes in dreams are sometimes good, other times, not so good. Wisdom, deceit, and sexual desire are some elements snakes represent. Carefully check the context of the dream.

People: Are they relatives or friends? If you know the people, what do they represent in your waking life—love, or perhaps jealousy?

Many times, we see people as reflections of ourselves, but pay close attention to what the person is doing in your dream. The key to what the symbol is portraying is the context in which that person appears and what they are doing. If you dream of having dinner with friends and the platter is passed to you with no food left, you likely feel that your companions are not nourishing you. This is about your friendships. If, on the other hand, you see a good friend beating his brother, you might ask yourself if you are being too hard on a sibling?

Physical appearance of people

- Teeth, hair, and personal appearance?
- Jewelry or other adornments, such as tattoos?
- Clothing?
- Known or unknown to you?

Locations

- East?
- West?
- North?
- South?
- Type of terrain?
- Known to you or unknown?
- Dangerous?
- Beautiful?

Houses or buildings

- Solid?
- Old?
- New?
- Crumbling?
- Known or unknown to you?
- What is inside?
- Furnished?
- Vacant?

Weather or season

- Stormy?
- Sunny?
- Dark?
- Cold?
- Warm?
- Comfortable?

Geography

- Rocky?
- Meadow?
- Flat?
- Hospitable?
- Inhospitable?
- Barren?

Animals

- Wild?
- Domesticated?
- Unusual?
- Friendly?
- Known to you, like a current or former pet?

Predominant colors or sounds

- Brilliant?
- Dark?
- Beautiful?
- Jarring?
- Unpleasant?
- Reminiscent of something from your past?

A deeper dive into dream symbols

After you write down your dream, respond to the prompts on the Dream Cypher to analyze your dream. Then, go back and pick out the symbols that occurred in your dream. Have you dreamed before of these symbols? If so, what were the circumstances? This exercise should begin to inform you of the symbol's significant meaning to your life.

Take note of what you think about the main symbols in your dreams. Are these symbols comforting or bewildering? The questions that follow take you on a deep dive into your dream symbols. These basic questions will help you understand what a symbol means to you. After analyzing the symbols, you may go back and fill in details about those symbols on the Dream Cypher.

People

Who are the people in your dream? Who is the main character? Is it you? And who is interacting with the main character? Do you know these people, or are they unknown in your waking life? Do they communicate with you in the dream? What do the people look like? How do you look? Are you younger or older than you are now?

Teeth, hair, and physical characteristics are all symbolic references. If your teeth are falling out in a dream, your self-image might be dangerously low. If your hair is radiant, maybe this means your "crowning beauty" is evident to everyone and you are attracting what you want into your life. If you dream of an injured arm or leg, your forward momentum in life is possibly impeded.

Vehicles

Write down any transportation, whether a golf cart, train, car, or bicycle. Who is driving the car? Is someone on the train with you? What are you doing in the vehicle? Can you easily steer the car, or is it not responding to your commands?

Roads or pathways

If you are traveling, what path are you taking? Is it a bumpy road or highway? Do you encounter a roundabout or roadblock? These are indications of your current life path. Do you want to change that trajectory? Ask for a smoother or better path before sleeping to help with insight into how to fix the path or steer onto a new course.

Locations

Is there a building, house, or school? Take note of the weather, season, and geography. If the dream takes place in a house, where is the location in the house—upstairs, downstairs, attic? Is the house luxurious or drab, tidy or cluttered?

Weather

If the weather is inclement, how is that of note to you? Are you living in stormy circumstances with your loved ones? Are you sad and gloomy, like a rainy day? Is it spring in your dream? Do you feel like everything is "coming up roses"?

Can you discern where the dream takes place? Is it in a specific country or region? Is it a rural or urban setting? Try to look for any other details related to the dream's setting.

Animals

What kind of animals appear in the dream? Are they domesticated pets? Or are they dangerous wild animals? Animals often are symbols of distilled characteristics of people you encounter in your waking life. A hawk may represent a person with a harsh, predatory demeanor—someone who watches you "like a hawk."

Animals might also represent your personal characteristics—faithful like a dog, clever and conniving like a raccoon, or fierce like a lion.

Colors or sounds

Does a certain color catch your attention? I once analyzed a dream in which the door of a house the person was entering was turquoise. I asked this dreamer what turquoise meant to him. He told me it was the color of the house he grew up in—an unusual color for a house, I admit. This dream symbol was trying to point out that a habit from childhood was still governing his behavior. The message was that he didn't have to walk through that door and behave that way anymore.

If a sound is predominant in your dream, what kind of sound is it—background noise, a song, a bell, a siren? All these symbols indicate your state of mind. A bell usually means something is calling for you, as bells call people together, like in churches or during times of trouble. A siren is a warning sound. A song is trying to give you a specific message related to its lyrics. Songs elicit emotional responses, offering succinct messages about your life circumstances. As an example, if the song "Beware of Darkness" shows up in a dream (or from seemingly out of nowhere in real life), that is a clear admonition about the danger of allowing negativity into your life either in the form of a person or an attitude.

Symbols bundle things up nicely so you can easily get the picture. The next chapter details the different dream types that are usually encountered. Once you figure out what kind of dream you had, and note its particular symbols, you are on your way to understanding your dreams' messages.

SECTION THREE

Dream Archetypes

CHAPTER ONE

UNDERSTANDING COMMON DREAM TYPES

Humans have several types of dreams because life involves several types of common problems. Psychiatrist Viktor Frankl, a concentration camp survivor, had the perspective that life needs meaning to be worthwhile. We are called to try to understand the meaning of these problems, and not merely attempt 'the discharge of tension at any cost' as Viktor Frankl admonishes against. We are all here for a purpose, and that particular purpose will have problems to unravel and meaning to be gained.

The common dream types help you make sense and bring meaning to your dreams. As I got deeper into my dreams, and had more years of practice writing them down, I realized that understanding my dreams takes a special kind of disciplined wisdom. You are likely to get some tough love served up along with the wisdom. If you find yourself wondering if that rather nasty dream about your mother-in-law hating you is true, this chapter is for you.

Don't fret over a fear dream by mistaking it for a precognitive dream, nor wonder if that dream of your flying around a circus in skimpy attire is indicative of your chosen path. These dreams are categorized to sort out the "take action immediately" from the "lighten up and enjoy life" types of dreams.

The first things to focus on are understanding the symbols your dream is using, and then, what kind of dream is it.

Types of dreams

To tell what kind of dream you just had and want more information on, start with a few simple questions. Are your dreams about lack, deception, or betrayal? Are you frequently getting lost? Is there some consistency to your dream themes?

Dreams can have several different interpretations so you can analyze them on several levels. To begin to sort them out, think of the types detailed in this chapter and the story each type of dream tells you. Dreams are private screenings of your life's themes that have good characters and bad characters as well as outcomes of potential actions that you might consider in your waking life.

Diverse types of dreams also have different personality infusions and feeling tones that permeate the dream. Think of it like a movie—the lighting is a feeling tone, and the musical score is a personality infusion. These subtleties are in every film. Your dreams have nuanced characteristics meant to help you understand the dream's significance to you.

This chapter is perfect for helping you discover what kinds of dreams you experience most and why you are getting that kind of information. These are the most common types of dreams:

- Problem-solving Dreams
- Warning Dreams
- Precognitive, Prophetic, or Visionary Dreams
- Past Life Dreams
- Dreams of Projected Fears
- Entertainment Dreams
- Soul Nourishment Dreams
- Soul Damage Dreams
- Life Path Dreams
- Clearinghouse Dreams

This chapter explains how you can discern what type of dream you just had and what to do with it. This is helpful, for example, if you incorrectly label a clearinghouse dream as a warning dream. Instead of changing your behavior as you might if you thought you were being warned of an upcoming situation, you realize that you are just clearing out some left-over stress. You will learn how to appropriately use the dream's information. The Basic Dream Cypher helps sort out your dreams and analyzes them as you go, so the dream material is available to your consciousness, and you can make decisions in real time. This book features real dreams from real people with real problems. You will learn how they used their dreams to achieve solution-based outcomes.

The Basic Dream Cypher Template is provided below.

BASIC DREAM CYPHER TEMPLATE

Write down the dream exactly as you remember it:

Tell the story of your dream by asking questions about the details of the symbols that were not in your first written version of the dream:

Take note of actions, directions, locations, and timing:

Describe the feeling-tone, and ignite your intuition by seeing if any thoughts come into your mind about this dream:

List the symbols observed in your dream:

Make note of current and relevant life events:

Take a moment for a reality check:

Write a brief conclusion:

If called for, make an action plan:

Give your dream a title and a date:

The following chapters supply more depth and detailed examples of the distinct dream archetypes.

• Problem Solving Dreams

This is the most popular and useful type of dream to help solve everyday problems. It's kind of like your favorite Uncle Jack, who comes around right when you need him and says, "I have just the person you should meet to help you with your problem."

You throw your arms around your uncle and say, "Thank goodness. You got here just in time. Whew!"

Uncle Jack looks at his feet and shyly says, "That's what I'm here for. Gotta go."

That's the low-key feeling-tone of a problem-solving dream. That's how you recognize it. There's no fanfare, no wild imagery. Just the facts, ma'am.

Sometimes, you get a call or have a conversation with someone within a few days of asking for a dream regarding a problem. Your intuition has been ignited, and now the solution is being made available.

• Warning Dreams

Unlike the subtle tones of problem-solving dreams, warning dreams have extremely specific feeling-tones that elicit strong emotions. The plot lines often feature specific people or a background personality you sense but don't see. Pay close attention to the outcomes of these dreams. Sometimes, the personality of the dream is so forthright that there is no confusion. You can almost hear these words in a warning dream: "This is what happens when you make a bad decision."

This kind of dream feels like an IRS officer has just knocked on your door and you're still in your jammies. For example, I once had a dream that I looked in the mirror and had the worst haircut ever. I couldn't even feel good about growing it out—it was that bad. Concurrently, I was negotiating a settlement with a company that had illegally diverted a lot of money from a joint escrow account. I distrusted the company president and didn't want to deal with him anymore, so I tentatively agreed to a pitifully small settlement for what my company was owed from the escrow account.

As much as I didn't want to deal with this person, I realized I wasn't ever going to like the outcome. A really bad haircut I couldn't even grow out well is a pretty bad outcome. I decided against agreeing to the settlement. I later negotiated a far more equitable agreement, but it wasn't easy or pleasant.

• Precognitive Dreams

Precognitive dreams appear as out-of-the-blue events unfolding before you. They are usually quite helpful, like someone you trust saying to you in your dream, "Oh, you might want to avoid that guy over there. He's a real jerk."

This feels like your best friend, who knows everything. For example, you may dream of a baby girl being born to you, and sure enough, later you have a baby girl. Your dream best friend just nods her head. "Of course," she says smiling, "I knew that."

• Prophetic Dreams

Prophetic dreams feel like someone you don't know—a kind stranger—has decided to show you something special. It's like finding a secret librarian in a mysterious castle—someone who knows about everything and has wisdom to impart. These dreams are usually emotionally charged and sometimes even fantastical. For example, I dreamed of a dangerous fog rolling over America and killing lots of animals and people in its wake. My baby horse, a beautiful black-and-white paint, was lying in the field, gasping for breath. My only recourse was to stay in the house.

This was 2008, and the fog in my dream represented the disinformation about financial derivatives and the effects they would have on businesses—in particular, the real estate business. Overnight, my business lost hundreds of millions of dollars in listings and clients. We shut down our offices and moved our headquarters to my house. We stayed inside the house, as the dream suggested.

That financial "fog" enshrouded the real world for a few years, and many businesses lost their viability. Our business, symbolized by the beautiful black-and-white paint horse in my dream, was a specialty niche business. It didn't fare well during the Great Recession.

• Visionary Dreams

A visionary dream is something altogether different from any other type of dream. These dream types are exceedingly rare and quite special. However, the personalities that might come through are sometimes deceptively simple. Usually the personality is unassuming, and yet has a quietly exceptional quality. Such personalities might open doors that appear in your dream where there were no doors. Or they might touch your hand to envelop you in a beautiful light. The feeling-tone of this dream has a magical quality.

My good friend, while recovering in the hospital, not quite awake, dreamed of a blue light surrounding him and his daughter, who coincidently, was sitting next to his bed and holding his hand while waiting for him to awaken. He marveled at how peaceful he felt. He felt everything was going to be simply fine. And it was.

• Past Life Dreams

Personalities that come through these dreams represent attributes you had during the lifetime that is being portrayed. If you were a stern, demanding personality in a past life, the dream shows you that personality. You will notice an aspect of yourself in a context you probably never thought about before.

Say you dream of a sequestered Russian wife, who looks stern and unhappy. You realize when you see her in your dream that you have felt stern and sequestered in your marriage. Knowing the problem has been with you for a while may help you overcome its grip on your perceptions of your life.

Or perhaps you dream of a warrior who lay dying in his heavy armor amid the outgoing tide. You realize you sometimes fight to the death even when the tide has turned, and it is time to shed the armor and lay down your sword. Past life dreams have a lot to teach us in this lifetime, so look for those messages.

• Warning Dreams

Warnings that come to you in dreams are usually very direct, don't use a lot of symbols, and have a current time frame.

Here is an example:

> *...A friend of mine was very mad at me. He said that I didn't act like I cared how his life was going and never called to even say hello.*

I realized that the dream was correct. I hadn't called him in a long while, and he had been a good friend to me over many years. I didn't realize that he would be hurt by my inaction. I called him right away.

There is usually no need to analyze simple warning dreams as they show up in the form of advice that's direct and to the point. Simple warning dreams are usually in response to a situation that is imminent. If the dream has personal symbols in it and an atmosphere of unease with a warning message, a major negative event is about to happen. This is indicative of a prophetic dream, that is also a warning dream. The main differences are in the scope of the dream information. Simple warning dreams are relegated to your personal life, prophetic dreams involve a much broader range, more people's lives, a larger geographic area or a huge cultural shift.

• Fear Dreams

Dreams of fears, whether they are something as viscerally disturbing as menacing spiders or about your beloved straying from you, are good for identifying and releasing irrational fears. If the dreams of fear are about a potential future event, take heed. Do a reality check to see if any current events might precipitate the outcome of the fear dream.

• Worry Dreams

Worry dreams present themselves like a busybody who tells you nobody is to be trusted, your dog has run away, and you will surely never get another date in your life. Yet, with patience, you will discern that this is just another one of those troublemaking rants that rattle around in your head. These dreams never quite seem like they have a true voice behind them—because they don't. Understand the worry dream as a means of relaying what your mental minions are running around repeating, not as definitive advice or projected outcomes.

• Entertainment Dreams

If your dream casts you as the heroine in a car chase scene or a performer flying on a trapeze over an applauding crowd, your soul is giving you a dream vacation. We all need an occasional respite from the serious side of life, and dreams provide that outlet when reality sometimes can't.

If you'd like to bring such dreams to life, think about what you can do to invite some of that entertainment into your everyday life. You'll be surprised to find lots of inspiration to enrich your life.

• Soul Nourishment Dreams

These dreams guide you on your life path by showing you a story rich with symbols of what your life looks like on a spiritual level. Yes, they are sometimes hard to understand and at times don't seem to be giving you much advice. They offer perspective.

Here is an example:

> *...I was riding on a huge, white horse. We could do anything, jump over cars, navigate bumpy roads. Anything. I felt very lucky to have such a horse. .*

These dreams feel like you are sitting on a beach and watching the waves of your life roll by. *Ahhh.*

• Soul Damage Dreams

As you might imagine, soul damage dreams are my least favorite type. If you are allowing someone in your life to cause you soul damage, these dreams show you exactly what kind of damage is being caused. Pay close attention to these dreams. Soul damage is not just a clever term. Real physical and emotional harm is happening to you.

A soul damage dream is a call for you to take control of your life. Immediately.

• Life Path Dreams

If you've ever wondered what you are meant to do with your life, these dreams provide scenarios, which are usually very subtle. They almost get lost in the more fantastical entertainment dreams or more helpful problem-solving dreams. Still, you will recognize them because they appear in conjunction with other types of dreams as a quiet, peaceful voice that often surprises you. Are you walking with a famous writer? That means you are walking the path of a writer. Are you getting advice from a successful businessperson? You are in the same bubble as that successful businessperson, doing what you are meant to do. Or, are you given a choice of roads in your dream? That means you are coming up on a choice of paths in life. Make better choices by paying attention to the paths your dreams present.

• Clearinghouse Dreams

Sometimes you just need to get rid of the detritus in your daily thoughts. Perhaps a coworker spoke harshly to you, your kids are eating you out of house and home, or your relatives are ruining your peace and calm with their demands. Or you're plain tired. (Note to self: time to reread Matthew Walker's *Why We Sleep*.) This type of dream clears out those tired thoughts to make way for more inspiration and rejuvenation.

CHAPTER TWO

SOLVING PROBLEMS THROUGH YOUR DREAMS

If you would like to request a dream but don't have a lot of facts, or don't know exactly what you want, this chapter shows how to ask for and interpret a scenario dream. Problems are part of everyday life. You could even say your approach to problems defines your life. So, how to solve problems to procure the best outcomes are often a primary focus for most of us. Why not use your dreams to help with this recurring lifelong task? Why not employ your embedded board of directors? Remember—your dreams always have your back.

Problem-solving dreams usually involve a feeling of working things out, and the story line likely has more than one possible outcome. I like problem-solving dreams best of all. They are easy to identify and to access information from. Here are the various forms in which problem-solving dreams deliver their services:

- **Insight into the Problem.** Some problem-solving dreams give insight so you can take appropriate action toward a solution. Or they help you get to the next step of asking for another dream once you understand the underlying problem.

- **Solution or Incubation Dreams.** These problem-solving dreams suggest actions you could take to correct or improve your current situation.
- **Scenario Dreams.** Problem-solving dreams that showcase a possible scenario could help you decide whether or not the scenario depicted is desirable or undesirable to you.
- **Character Insight.** These problem-solving dreams show you the personality or characteristics of a person you would like to better understand or who has a role in the problem you are trying to solve.

Here's the Problem-Solving Dream Template:

PROBLEM SOLVING DREAM CYPHER TEMPLATE

Write down your question, thinking about how to best frame the question:

Make notes of any issues associated with your question. Ask for dreams that offer insight about all of the facets of the issue:

Tell the story of your dream:

Describe the feeling-tone of the dream:

List the symbols observed in your dream:

Jot down current events, including signs you've recently noticed:

Do a reality check:

Write a brief conclusion by rewriting what the actual problem was and what the dream solutions seemed to indicate:

Make a potential action plan. What are your options-pros and cons:

Give your dream a title and a date:

To supplement your use of the Problem-Solving Dream Cypher template, here are some additional suggestions about the process to gain insight into solving your issue:

1) Write down a question you have about a nagging problem, thinking about how to best frame the question.

Let's start with the premise that you have a library of solutions for all of your problematic issues. First, you need to decide what the issue is and what you want to do with it. Picture yourself going into that library and looking for a book about...well, what? Your question needs to have some specificity. You can't just stand in front of a shelf and ask for solutions regarding something vague, like stress or anxiety. You must narrow it down.

A very practical application for accessing your inner dream wisdom is to ask for insight about a particular person or situation. For example, you might ask, "Is this job going to be in my best interest and for my higher purpose right now?" Whether you write it down in your Dream Workbook or recite it aloud, the point is to be very clear about what information you are requesting.

Be very honest with yourself in pinpointing problems. Specifically, what is the issue? Broad questions draw broad answers. If, say, you feel stressed, you need to know what is really causing you the stress in order to get an answer for that problem. If you are under stress and think the issue is job-related, ask yourself if quitting your job and getting another is a viable option. If it's not that simple, then asking for a dream to gain more insight is a solid first step.

The reasons you have certain problems may be rooted in your acceptance of the tenets of the problem. So, to get the best information from a dream, you need to get to the root of the issue. Let's say your job stresses you out, but you believe you can't quit because you need the money—you are falsely accepting that your current job is the only job possible to provide your income. Of course, that probably isn't the case, so why do you feel that way? If you ask for a dream on how to relieve the job-related stress, you may get a dream about going on vacation.

But what you really want is more money. The stress is coming from not quite having enough income, you think. You'd like a job that earns more. But you don't quit your current job because you are afraid a higher-paying job means less time at home with your children. So, the problem really involves time, not just money. Now you can begin to solve the time and money problem and ask for a useful dream.

Try this question for dream insight: "What kind of job situations would provide me with sufficient income and time to be with my children?" My point is that problems can be slippery. Before you ask for a useful dream, know the genuine issues. Really think about what information would be helpful.

2) Be fully clear about all the issues around your solution-seeking question.

As noted, state your question specifically to get the best answer—or multiple answers, since sometimes it takes a few dreams for you to develop a plan. For those of you who want to be warned about what's ahead, you don't need to ask for a warning dream to solve your problem. Warning dreams tend to show up on their own. Unless you suspect an adverse situation might arise, is it inadvisable to ask for a warning dream. Don't unnecessarily drum up fear.

For example, I had a dream of a baby who died. I wasn't sure in the dream if the baby was a boy or girl. I wasn't being warned of a miscarriage—I didn't need to be fearful about that. The symbol of the baby referred to a business I had just started, not yet a fully formed "boy or girl," just a business I realized was going to tank due to lack of funding. I was sad but not devastated, as I would expect to be with the death of a baby. This told me my heart was not fully invested in this business.

As you can see, the story and characters may change (boy or girl?), or even the outcome might change as you are dreaming. Many times, the story evolves as you dream, and upon waking, you have the solution. Problem-solving dreams have many subtle variations. Lots of people report having gone to bed with a problem and waking up with a solution, but not remembering a dream at all.

Problem-solving dreams are also quite practical and to the point. You will feel as if your grandmother were chatting with you. "Just get on with it," she says. When I say dreams have personalities, I mean it. That's why the Dream Cypher template has questions to uncover the subtleties in dreams. First ask yourself how you felt when dreaming the dream. Did you feel like you were just observing? Or were you in the dream? Make good observations. You will become much more observant than you were at first. You use not only your conscious mind, but also your subconscious mind, to access your dream observations.

Now ask yourself, when you were observing, did you feel like the colors or sounds were vibrant, like you were watching a movie? Or was the feeling-tone more like a black-and-white movie—not very colorful nor overly dramatic? Was the movie exciting or did it feel like just another day at the office? That's what I mean by the feeling-tone of a dream. Making note of what kind of emotion you felt while watching this movie your subconscious mind generated is your first indication of what your dream is trying to communicate with you.

Understanding of the finer characteristics of the dream comes a bit later, after you have recorded and looked at your dreams for a while. Some dreams are playful and funny—maybe inside jokes only you understand, like how much you love licorice or that red convertible you sold years ago.

Some dreams are admonitions. These usually have a family member who reprimands you for eating the wrong food or dating that person who is fun but not dependable. Some dole out advice from the chairman of your dream board—more businesslike, less friendly, not funny, and just laying it out for you.

I believe that if you follow your inner guidance, you can find a way out of all problems. Like entrepreneur Marie Forleo says, "Everything is figureoutable." By the way, I highly recommend her book by the same name, *"Everything is Figureoutable."* I am a huge fan of this author because I believe, as she does, that every problem has a solution. I would add that dreams help in mining those solutions.

3) Ask more specific questions:

Don't vaguely ask, for example, if a person or situation is good for you. What does "good for me" mean to you? You might believe "good for me" translates to being with a partner who is financially successful. But what if that partner is also dismissive and demeaning of your kids? That would cause another kind of stress.

Try this question instead: "Please show me the kind of person this partner will really be to me and my children?" You are now asking for an insight dream. Or, if this is a business situation and you want to know whether the promotion to another department is better for your career, instead of asking, "Is this job better for me?" you might ask, "Does the job in the other department serve my highest and best purpose right now?" Or "Will I like the working environment in the new department?"

4) Ask for dreams that offer insight about characters or situations.

Clarify the question you want to ask, and if you are writing it down in your Dream Workbook, make the intent of the question as straightforward as possible. Rewrite the question until it is clear, if necessary. If you don't get a dream after the third night, rethink your question and consider rephrasing it. The purpose of writing down your question is to make sure you ask the right question in the right way. You don't need to put it under your pillow. After you've written it down and have the question in your mind, just think about it before you go to sleep.

If you don't get an answer, you may be asking a question with a lot of potentially conflicting answers. In that case, look carefully at how you have written the question. Or maybe you are already getting answers—through intuition, daydreams, unexpected phone calls, random meetings, or titles on a bookshelf. Because dreams ignite your intuition, answers may come in different vehicles instead of just dreams. You can double-check your intuition through your dreams as well, but more on that later.

5) What can you do right now to solve this problem? Keep thinking about it. Make a note about how you would do this.

If you think working with your dreams means you are off the hook for forward momentum, stop right now. Dreams provide guidance, wisdom, and a peaceful space to think things through and come up with the right solution. Calories are required! You must ultimately be active about solving your problems. Dreams rarely give you a one-and-done solution. Dreams usually give insight for you to see a situation more clearly, and then it's up to you to take appropriate action.

Problem-solving dreams can also be insight dreams, the difference being that the dreamer is asking for guidance on a specific situation within the context of a problem-solving dream. An insight dream sets forth an issue with truthful insight so your conscious mind can solve the problem in a way you deem best.

Life's dilemmas can stem from an incomplete or erroneous understanding of what the problem is. This is why insight into a problem or issue is the front runner of true problem-solving. Several types of dreams can help you solve problems.

First, you must know what the problem really is. Is it a relationship problem disguised as a work problem? Or is a perspective problem disguised as a money problem? Or is it perhaps that a situation problem is disguised as a marital problem? It helps to know what you really want from a dream—besides solving the problem for you! I'm reminded of the Rolling Stones song, "You Can't Always Get What You Want."

6) Leave space on the Dream Cypher template to go back and record your current life's events, including signs you recently noticed. Use the Problem-Solving Dream Cypher for Incubation, Scenario Dreams.

If you use the Dream Cypher template regularly you can keep track of your life's events and the efficacy of your dreams. You will learn to recognize and ask better questions, so your dreams will answer more specifically. Once you have analyzed a dream as best you can, leave it alone for a bit. Usually, you begin to see signs in your daily life that reinforce a decision or confirm that you are on the right track. This might sound challenging, but it really isn't.

Let me give an example of how a dream and a sign might work together. I was once going through a mid-career crisis. (Only once? Lucky me.) I had asked for a dream about which direction to go: how should I earn money? I had the idea that my real estate skills would still be useful, but I didn't know how. I no longer had a viable business. I had no staff, and my previous niche, which was resort real estate sales, didn't have a viable market in the new economy that dipped after 2008. Also, I had a decidedly negative attitude toward lots of travel, having done it for many years. So, I recorded my thoughts and waited for some direction.

7) Watch for clues in your waking life.

I was taking a shower, and I suddenly remembered my cousin's friend had a real estate franchise in my town. I didn't remember his name, but I thought, *what if there are large projects here, I could help with? I wouldn't have to board a plane or recruit sales agents in remote locations.* These thoughts just rolled out of my head and onto a mental cookie sheet. These ideas just might become half-baked cookies. *What to do now?* Time for a reality check.

8) Do a reality check and ask for specifics.

"Education consists mainly of what we have unlearned."
Mark Twain

Check to see how you might pull off the idea gleaned from your dream. Is it an ideal solution? Is it unusual or unconventional? What might you do differently? Write down the pros and cons of your dream guidance, and what you might do to make the idea a reality. Ask yourself if the solution derived from your dream is what you really want. If enough of a foundation is in place, then it is time to take that next step of reflection.

9) Reflect on your dreams and the solutions they offer.

"It's not what happens to you, but how you react to it that matters."
Epictetus

This step is important—but can seem unimportant while in the throes of a problem. At this point, you've been specific and have refined your request. You've received a dream, or maybe even a few dreams. You've also done that reality check, so now is the time for reflection, the hesychia.

When I talk about reflection to someone who has asked for dreams about specific problems, I often get a blank look. "Why?" they ask. "Isn't it time for action?"

Yes…and no.

I use the term, hesychia, to describe taking a moment to be with yourself and think deeply on whether you are ready to move forward. Even if the path you're on is your preferred route, is it the one you're meant to travel?

Give yourself time to think about what it is *you* are asking for. Take note of what worked before and what didn't. Make mental notes of better questions you could have asked or alternate actions you could have taken. Sometimes, in this period of reflection, you get a dream that further refines your thinking. Other times, you get deeper insight to help you move forward. All actions have reactions, so be sure and confident of your choices.

Hesychia—that moment in time to reflect and purify your thoughts—can bring more insight, joy, course correction, and confidence. Don't discount it. Take a moment. When you feel peaceful, that is a signal to move to the next step.

10) Write a brief conclusion by rewriting what the actual problem was that you stated in the above question and what the dream solutions seemed to indicate:

Life is messy and not all endings are successful conclusions. Or maybe I should say most endings are not really endings at all. They just seem like it. Your dreams can be part of the arsenal you have to make the most of your life and your life aspirations. You are allowed to change your mind, as I will illustrate in upcoming chapters. Dreams can help with understanding the opportunities, like I have just illustrated, or taking full advantage of financial opportunities, or understanding who people really are. It's all about learning to make better choices based on better questions and better information.

11) Make a potential action plan. What are your options-pros and cons?

This doesn't have to be a big plan or even the final plan. Just the practice of making a plan based on your insight is good practice. Practice and perfect.

12) Give your dream a title and a date:

Be Patient

Don't expect change overnight. Dreams are not your fairy godmothers. They are pointers to help you navigate your life in conjunction with your unique abilities and proclivities.

Now that you have the process down, let's apply it to the several types of dreams that occur as problem-solving dreams. To refresh your memory, here are the different types of dreams for problem-solving:

1. Insight into Others
2. Insight into Situations
3. Incubation Dreams
4. Scenario Dreams

The next chapters do a deep dive into these specific types of dreams.

CHAPTER THREE

INSIGHT INTO OTHERS

Asking for character insight

As you might imagine, understanding the character of others is very tricky. Both asking for unbiased insight and then making sure that the insight given is correctly interpreted. We are all subject to our almost immediate first impression of likes and dislikes of other people. Most of our reactions to others aren't built upon real insights into their character. Sometimes, instead, they are based on a supposition that the person has a contribution to make to our lives. Or, we have a contribution to make to theirs. Or our personalities are compatible under the current circumstances.

The key to character insight is combining insight about the person with the situational context of their behavior. So, asking for insight into someone's character without also asking for insight into the circumstances surrounding the intersection with your life is to underestimate the importance of context. In that sense, dreams for situational insight and dreams for character insight sometimes overlap.

Asking for a dream about a person's character is risky business in my experience. Insight into the character someone exhibits as related to the context of the relationship will likely lead you to better understanding the *circumstances* that might influence their behaviors. That is useful information.

That is also why you may get dreams that seem to involve dramatic circumstances even if all you asked was, "Is this person I'm dating good marriage material?"

The answer is usually, "That depends on the circumstances." If you want real insight, it helps to be objective, realistic, and, later, compassionate if necessary.

Using the Problem-Solving Dream Cypher Template, here are the preliminary steps:

1. Have a relaxed, calm attitude. Sometimes these dreams do not dole up the information you expect.
2. Be sure to ask for the best insight about the circumstances surrounding all of the parties, so you can make the best current choices for your life.
3. If you are asking for insight about your child, then build in a lot of love and empathy for yourself and your child. This might be difficult if you are the target of an angry teenager or a stepchild who feels misplaced, but a bit of love may smooth the way.
4. Be very clear with your question, as discussed in the previous chapter.
5. If your dream delivers an ambiguous answer, rephrase the question, and ask again.

An example of character and circumstance insight

The backstory:

A young woman was considering a marriage proposal from her boyfriend. She asked for a dream about what kind of marital partner he would be in a marriage. She was a very practical young woman, who wanted an emotionally solid and financially responsible partner. This was her dream:

An Unstable Foundation

...A man, who I thought was my husband, was building a house. He didn't have the money, so he was getting a loan through a third party. First, he put up one pole. Then he put up another, slightly crooked and not in line with the first pole.

I said to him, "Usually, I see that a whole side is framed and then the other whole side is framed, and the two sides are raised and fastened together. The same process for the opposite two sides, not one pole at a time. Those poles look crooked, and I don't think they will hold together."

But he wouldn't listen. He was angry and insistent that he knew how to build a house and I didn't. Soon, there was a whole line of crooked poles erected but not fastened together. They looked very unstable, not like a house structure at all. He said, "There, it looks good to me."

I disagreed. "No, not really," I said. "They look like they will fall over." Just then, the whole batch of poles fell over, just as I expected they would. Then, the money from the third party fell through to build the house. My "husband" got angrier and angrier. Apparently, the man who was going to loan the money did not know it was for a house. The foundation of the house was a disaster and not usable.

Let's break it down.

Problem Solving Dream Cypher (Expanded version)

Write down the dream exactly as you remember it. If you have a question, write it down, thinking about how to best frame the question. Make notes of any issues associated with your question. Ask for dreams that offer insight about all of the facets of the issue:

Does this man have the ability to 'build a house' with me? In real life, she realized that she needed some clarity about what life would be like with this man. Not just financially, but emotionally. She wanted to know about his long-term vision of marriage and whether she would enjoy living with him. Specifically, she wanted life to be peaceful and he seemed to enjoy squabbling.

Tell the story of your dream:

When this dreamer relayed the story to me, she said that during the dream she was concerned about the boyfriend's ability to build a foundation, both emotionally and financially. She was also perplexed about his true financial situation. When recounting the dream as a story, she remarked about how unstable this house was. Crooked poles. A poorly thought-out building plan. A shady loan. An unpleasant, chaotic atmosphere.

Take note of actions, directions, locations, and timing:

"It seemed like it was a current event. The whole scene revolved around building the house. I couldn't tell if the location was one I recognized, it didn't stand out as anything unusual."

Describe the feeling-tone of the dream:

"The whole atmosphere was disorganized and a bit desperate," this dreamer said.

A feeling-tone is useful for getting to the overall impression of the situation. For those people who have feelings that are not expressed in their verbiage concerning a dream, a feeling-tone clarifies the true message of the dream. In this case, this young woman has a deep need for organization and structure. Identifying the feeling-tone of disorganization and desperation showed her that life with this man would likely be filled with those characteristics.

List the symbols observed in your dream:

Building a house is a symbol of building a life together. Crooked poles symbolize unstable support. The source of money that disappeared or wasn't forthcoming indicates lack of financial stability. The structure collapsing is an indication of a future divorce or a relationship that is not stable.

Make note oof current and relevant life events. What is a major issue to you at this time? Include any signs you've recently noticed:

They didn't live together however he didn't seem to be interested in any repairs on her house. Also, he had never mentioned what kind of house he might like to buy. She realized she really didn't know anything about what kind of lifestyle he wanted. She hadn't noticed anything unusual but just felt something was off.

Take a moment for a reality check:

Her dream matched the reality of what she was observing. She wasn't surprised.

Note that sometimes the reality check will not match the dream material. If that is the case, it's time to ask for another dream for clarification.

Write a brief conclusion by rewriting what the actual problem was that you stated in the above question and what the dream solutions seemed to indicate:

The actual problem went beyond what she was asking about. Her question was whether this man could make a 'solid foundation.' But the surrounding issues of preferred lifestyle, his available resources, their combined capabilities and his interest in caring for and maintaining a house became apparent. The dream strongly indicated his lack of planning and resources.

Make a potential action plan. What are your options-pros and cons?

It seemed very obvious to her that she needed to ask more questions before agreeing to buy a house with him. She realized her assumptions about caring for a house were not necessarily what his assumptions were. A solid foundation involved much more than just buying a house together, in her opinion.

Let your intuition drive your action plan. Here's what this dreamer relayed to me about her final thoughts on the matter: "I shouldn't marry him and expect that I alone can build emotional or financial stability.

If I want to marry and build something, this man is not my partner for that. He's fun, and if all I wanted was to date that would be fine. If I want stability, that's not in his skill set.

Give your dream a title and a date:
An Unstable Foundation. 2.22.24

Character insight

What about a lover, would-be husband, future wife, or current partner? This dream was from a young woman dating a young man who wanted to see her exclusively. She was reluctant about the relationship. Her intuition told her something was off. She experienced a straightforward personality insight dream:

Shipwrecked

> *...I was stranded on a beach, and there was the CFO of the company I worked for. He was grumpily saying he had to live under a rock with me. Our vessels had been shipwrecked. I looked at the rock and realized it was dark and not that roomy. I didn't want to live under that rock with him. I didn't even like him that much.*

I asked this dreamer about the CFO at her place of employment. Did she work with him a lot? Yes, she did, and she found him to be a very difficult person. He was very crabby and sarcastic in his tone. Had the CFO always been like that? No, he seemed a lot nicer when she first met him in the context of the company. I asked if she wanted to date him. She said, "Absolutely not." He was much older and didn't seem at all interested in her or interesting to her. She didn't have much personal contact with the CFO outside of work.

So, if the dream wasn't referring to the CFO, could his character represent her current boyfriend? Was her boyfriend anything like the CFO? As it turned out, her boyfriend was a CPA, just like the CFO. And her current boyfriend was a bit grumpy and sarcastic. "In fact, sometimes he seems quite mean-spirited," she said.

"And he didn't seem like that when you were first dating?" I asked.

"No," she said, "he was a lot of fun in the beginning."

Hmmm. "Well, are you keeping it quiet that you are dating him—like 'under a rock'?"

"Yes," she sheepishly admitted, she explained that she wasn't quite divorced yet and didn't want to *rock* the boat with her soon-to-be ex-husband. Note that she used the word "rock."

I believed the dream was telling her the boyfriend was grumpy about not being acknowledged publicly. He didn't like being hidden "under a rock." Underneath the rock was a dark and small place, and it was possible his home might exhibit similar characteristics. He had personality traits like those of the CFO, who was also a grumpy guy. She didn't like the CFO at all once she had gotten to know him. The shipwreck—a disaster—was an indication of her life with the new boyfriend. None of the indicators in the dream were positive for this relationship.

I followed up with her some months later. She was still dating him. He had told her he felt like he was being kept "under a rock." Yes, he used that phrase. No, he didn't know about the dream. And no, she hadn't yet introduced him to her family. In addition, he had a very small, barren apartment she didn't like at all. "Like the space under the rock?" I asked her a little bit wryly.

She said, "Yes, just like living under a rock." She said she felt "shipwrecked" with him—"stranded and not going anywhere." This was not at all what she wanted in her life. "And," she added, "he is very moody. Sometimes he is sweet and caring, and then he will be sarcastic and biting in his comments about me." In the meantime, she had several dreams in which the boyfriend was trying to get her to rob a bank. In another dream, the boyfriend pushed her out of a window. *None* of her dreams conveyed positive messages about this relationship.

When she finally broke up with him, she said it was because he was just too mean-spirited and bullying toward her. Nothing seemed ever to work out with their plans and that made her feel that life with him would be a series of failed dreams. The most challenging element of character insight dreams is that sometimes the insight doesn't match our desires or expectations.

Business partners

Dreams about business associates are easier to decipher than those about loved ones. Usually, business partners are not as emotionally connected. The following dream examples feature a group of men who had been golf buddies for years. They were not exactly business partners, but they relied on one another for business advice. All three of these dreams are from one of these men:

An Unreliable Riding Partner

...My friend and potential business partner called to ask if he could come over to ride horses with me. I said sure, although he had never ridden before as far as I knew. He arrived and immediately went out to ride with my wife. I asked him why he didn't wait for me, and he said he just wanted to ride with her. I was surprised and a bit hurt because I thought he wanted to have a professional relationship with me. It turned out he just wanted a social relationship and not even necessarily with me.

Never Enough to Go Around

...I was invited to a dinner with my golf partners. They ordered large quantities of food, and it was being passed around the table. It was Mediterranean food. When the food got to me, the dish was empty. This happened several times.

Drinks on the House, Except for Me

...My golf buddies and I went into a bar, and drinks were ordered all around. Once again, every time a drink was ordered, one never arrived for me.

This man had three dream experiences in which he did not get the same treatment as the other men, who were supposed to be his friends and mentors. Three experiences that reap the same result is a demonstration of the dream-self emphasizing the information's importance. Always take note of the repetition of any three symbols or circumstances.

The dream also showed his friends really didn't care about riding (a symbol of creating a partnership) with him, having dinner with him (forging a profitable business relationship), or sharing drinks with him (having an interest in social interactions).

In Conclusion

Pay attention to the behavior of the person in the context of the dream circumstances. When a dream has information that seems unlikely, take heed, and ask your question again, or ask another question to confirm the information from the dream. The series of dreams noted above indicate that this man's relationship with his friends might not have a solid business base, or even a social base or any kind of caring interaction one would expect from good friends.

This doesn't mean the man should not have those friends. The dreams put those particular friends into a context for him. They are golf buddies, nothing more.

CHAPTER FOUR

INSIGHT INTO SITUATIONS

One way to create the life you want is to understand the situations you find yourself in. Then you can do something about it. This is where insight into situations comes in handy.

For example, once I asked for insight into how to get promoted and earn more money at one of my first jobs. I asked if I might get a promotion and a raise, but I received no dream answer. Then I asked if I would be financially stable in my current situation. Below is an account of the dream I had.

Descending Slowly

> *...I was on a large commercial airplane, which was descending slowly. I was wearing a beautiful coat, and I wanted to keep it on. I asked the flight attendant if I could keep it with me so I could get off the plane with it. She said, "I'm not sure you can keep it if you get off the plane. But, yes, you can keep it with you during the flight., Then she admonished me. "I hope you're not going to buy another expensive coat." The plane landed smoothly. I think I got to keep the coat on.*

Oh, no. I realized I was being advised that the company I worked for was descending, not going up. I was surprised by this because the company was the new offshoot of a very large, profitable corporation. I couldn't believe it.

But within six months, massive layoffs were made to everyone's surprise—except mine. I had been notified in my dream that the plane was going down and not up. Although I experienced the dream, I wasn't focused on the company's financial health, which I took for granted. I was instead focused on getting a promotion and a raise. I didn't understand how a well-funded company could be subject to layoffs for no apparent reason. But that's exactly what happened.

Also, the beautiful coat was my personal symbol of luxury. I was being advised in the dream not to buy another. The dream told me I should be frugal in the near term and not to spend any money on luxuries. The coat I had with me was safe, according to the flight attendant, but if I tried to get off the plane (quit my job) and planned to buy another one, that future action was advised against. So, my current prosperity was stable, as the coat was still mine, but the future was uncertain.

I followed the advice to avoid spending extravagantly. The dream also advised me that leaving the company might not be as prosperous for me, either. The dream anticipated my question about securing a better job to make more money. Obviously, that didn't look very good. The landing was smooth, though. That was the good news. Real-life events that transpired afterwards proved the dream's forecast to be accurate. There were layoffs, but I wasn't laid off. I didn't get a big raise, but I got a minor promotion and a small raise. The landing was smooth, after all.

I had another dream about that situation. I was trying to ascertain if I would keep my job after the massive layoffs. I was pregnant in real life, so I needed the benefits, not to mention the salary. I requested a meeting with the vice president of the division in which I worked, but he didn't have the time or inclination to talk to me. He barely knew me, so I could understand his behavior. He had just been promoted from his position as VP of sales, so he was being bombarded from every angle. I asked for a dream to have a talk with the VP of the division to see if I was going to keep my job. I got this dream:

Mr. C Agrees to Talk

...Mr. C, my division's VP, agreed to meet me and talk for a few minutes. He sat on the far end of the bench. He wasn't very friendly, but he wasn't terribly unfriendly either. I asked him if I would be considered for a director position in the company after the restructuring. He told me there wasn't any availability for that job. He wanted to go right away—he had a lot of work do. He said, "I like you. We'll see." But he got up and left. I felt he didn't want to commit to anything. Then, he disappeared.

I was disappointed in the VP's response in my dream, but he didn't say I wasn't going to have a job—just that I wouldn't get the director position. I realized I should have structured a more specific set of questions. I could have asked for my dream to clarify the question of keeping my current job and additionally about the promotion to director's position.

I waited and worried. A few weeks later, all of us in the marketing department were asked to go one by one into the VP's office. I was called in last. Either I was going to be the last one fired or the last person standing with a job. Everyone who came out of the VP's office was solemn and sullen. And they were not talking. They all said they couldn't discuss anything and proceeded back to their cubicles. The Director of Marketing started packing his boxes. Bad sign. I walked into the VP's office and sat down. Mr. C said, "We have decided not to have Directors in this division anymore. However, we are promoting you to Group Manager. You can move into the former Director's office, effective immediately."

It was a mixed blessing. It was both a surprise and a relief for me, but for many of my friends it was a very sad day overall. People everywhere were packing boxes and lumbering out the door. Most of the marketing department was laid off. My former boss was also laid off. I was now the group manager of four people, including myself. It was a skeleton crew of what we used to have.

My dream was correct. The VP had not lied to me. There wasn't a director position but a group manager position. I got a promotion, and the job lasted until the next restructuring a few years later. I got better about framing my questions after that.

Often, insight into a situation begins with insight into how and what you think about the people in that situation—not others' true characters but instead what we presume about their characters. Asking for the truth sometimes means facing the truth that you might have inaccurate opinions about others. Your reaction toward someone might be a displaced emotional response on your part.

CHAPTER FIVE

INCUBATION OR
SOLUTION DREAMS

I love the idea of incubation dreams. You ask for a solution, and you get an answer. Sounds simple, right? While I'm very fond of the idea, that's not how it always works in my practical experience. You don't always get simple answers. You may just get more insight. You might need to ignite your intuition so you can see an answer right in front of you—or even several steps ahead of you. Perhaps there are some lessons you need to learn along the way before you get to an answer.

Very irritating, I admit—and sometimes slower than one might wish. While I believe you will always get guidance, all of life's problems are not solved by the simple act of dreaming up a solution. Some problems are solved by following pebbles of solutions, one step at a time—informed by dreaming, and led by intuition and curiosity.

When your intuition is alerted to possibility, that provides you with information you may not have known exists or draws to you the resources needed to solve your problems. We all have issues that come up because of who we are and what we are here to learn. Some issues just take time to resolve through our everyday actions.

Incubation dreams are usually short and specific. Still, several such dreams might be necessary to solve a complicated issue. If the answer requires layers of explanation or has several parts to it, scenario dreaming is more appropriate. Scenario dreams, covered in a later chapter, usually appear because the issue involves more than a simple solution and there are several possibilities.

How to get answers from incubation dreams

Once, I had a specific question about quickly obtaining more cash in my business. My question was, "What can I do that will put more cash in my business within the next thirty days? I wanted to wait out the cash-flow crisis and not do anything rash, such as laying off needed staff members. Unfortunately, that would have been the simple but wrong solution. This was my dream:

A Tight Squeeze

>...*My big draft horse, named Bud Light, was squeezing under the barn door. I realized I needed to cut down on his food so he could lose weight and get into the barn. Otherwise, he wouldn't be able to get into the barn at all and could die of weather exposure if left outside.*

Draft horses equal workhorses in my dream symbology. If the workhorses (workers) couldn't get under the door. If he couldn't get into the barn, the workhorse might perish, indicating maybe the food (or salaries) represented too much overhead for the company to survive.

Does this mean I needed to scale down on salaries or personnel? Yes. Could I have figured that out on my own? Of course. But the dream made it crystal clear what I needed to do (and fast)—the one thing I was avoiding. I had to cut down on overhead. The overweight horse was an overhead issue. I had been trying to wait out the slow cash flow, but the dream persuaded me to rethink my strategy. Waiting would have been disastrous. The whole business might have gone under, as indicated by an inability to get into the barn.

Another example is a dream I had in 2009. Those of us in business then remember that year very well. It was like falling off a cliff, smacking the water hard, then sinking to the bottom and finding deep, dark sea creatures hungrily eyeing you.

Stuck Red Truck

...I was in the driver's seat of my red truck, stuck in an underground parking lot. Lots of cars and trucks were down there. None of us could move. I realized we were going to starve or die of thirst if we couldn't get our trucks out of there. I began to move a little bit, then another small turn, and then another and another. After much maneuvering and patience, I finally got the truck away from the main bunch of cars and trucks and could see the driveway that led to the upper floors of the parking lot.

Here's the backstory:

My business at the time was in resort real estate, and we were circling the economic drain. Suddenly, that second home in Costa Rica seemed like two concrete blocks tied to one's feet while walking a plank. Our clients, the developers, were going into bankruptcy, and buyers were desperately trying to get their money back. All new development business ground to a halt. The phone literally stopped ringing.

We shut down all our offices in several countries and states. We moved the remaining staff to our ranch, and we hunkered down. We hoped to wait for a resurgence in resort projects and meanwhile get the banks to let us sell inventory they had taken back from the developers. It was a bleak strategy, but I didn't have a better one. The main problem was that our bank had called our line of credit—insisting we pay off the whole balance, not due to any missed payments but because it no longer wanted the risk. Meantime the developers of the resort projects froze their assets, including our commissions.

We needed the cash to pay off the line of credit at the bank and to retain our remaining employees. The bank, which shall remain nameless because of its very bad behavior, kept all the commissions we had in the form of cash in the bank. We had hoped to make payments to the bank, keep our employees on payroll, and squeak by until the economy began to recover. No such luck.

My plan wasn't going to work. I didn't know what to do, whom to call, or how to salvage any commissions or retained earnings, or even attract new prospective business. In fact, I considered bankruptcy as the best possible solution to take the pressure off. That was a very distasteful proposition, because I loved being in business and knew from consulting a bankruptcy attorney that my credit would be ruined for years. I wouldn't be able to buy a house, get another line of credit, or even finance a car purchase. In short, I might not ever be able to start another business. I had fearful nightmares of being homeless. (I will get to fear dreams a little later.)

I asked for a dream to give me some direction: "Should I just claim bankruptcy? Can I get any new business? Could I get a job? What should I do and what direction could I take for the highest and best outcome to this problem and for the rest of my life?" That was my question and my request for a dream.

Now, here's what the "Stuck Red Truck" dream cited above told me. I knew if I maneuvered a bit here and a bit there, I could at least see a way out. I didn't get an answer to the way out of the garage—just enough for me to not give up, along with the promise that I could see the way out if I kept maneuvering. So, I did. Here was my action plan:

- I made a deal with the bank that I would remit small monthly payments if they withdrew the lawsuit, which was draining my cash.
- I went back to my clients and asked which banks had taken over their projects.
- I contacted those banks with the help of the developers and propositioned the banks that I would market and sell their projects for half of what I had charged before and forego the previously owed commissions—my twice-the-work-for-half-the-money offer.
- We would then sell the inventory for a price that would make the bank solvent on the deal—keeping the banks out of the clutches of the FDIC—and salvage the project for the developers as best we could, all the while earning enough for our company to stay afloat.

Politician John Sununu said, "A good compromise is one where everyone is a little unhappy." Those were "a little unhappy times." But just a little. Mostly, we were all a little happy as well. Maybe the new clients were little happy because they got to buy resort properties at lower prices, and I was a little happy because once again I was able to earn money and pay off my line of credit at a sustainable rate. Banks were slightly happy to keep the FDIC at bay. So, a good compromise.

Do you see how that dream worked? My truck was a symbol of my working life. The red truck was a vehicle, or the method by which I accomplished work. The truck being red indicated I could still sell some flashy products. I was working a little flamboyantly, hence the red color, but by edging my way out of that underground parking lot, I could make my way to a path that had upper levels, which represented more profitable possibilities. The dream gave me hope that if I kept maneuvering, I would succeed. I full-on went for it.

Now for a word or two about faith—in this case, faith in a dream that gives you direction for your future. What if you're wrong in your dream interpretation? A small decision would be survivable, but what about one that risks your entire future on a dream? I get that. I didn't want to fail either. I didn't want to keep trying only to potentially lose everything anyway.

So, let's employ a Russian strategy: trust but verify. Keep asking for dream guidance. I continued to ask questions along the way. I kept maneuvering, taking every little step and dealing with what was in front of me. Then, I checked on the results. If they were good, I kept doing what I was doing. If they were ambiguous, I asked for another dream.

For example, a relative of mine named Ron is a builder. He reported to me that he doesn't remember his dreams, but he often has construction problems he doesn't know how to solve but upon waking, he has solutions perfectly laid out for him. This is another way dreams work. They trigger your natural intuition by laying out the groundwork while you are sleeping that triggers a solution that comes to you after waking. That is the beauty of recording both your dream thoughts and waking thoughts. Once the barrier between waking life and sleeping life is relaxed, your intuition and synchronicity in life fills in the blanks for you to take the next steps.

CHAPTER SIX

SCENARIO DREAMING

If you would like to request a dream but don't have a lot of facts around a situation, don't know exactly what you want, or have chosen a path that is not working out, here's how to deal with that. This chapter is about asking for and interpreting a scenario dream. The purpose of a scenario dream is to give you options and insight into your current situation. Once again, use the Problem-Solving Dream Cypher Template.

This type of dream helped me after I began negotiations on a joint venture agreement with a large company to set up an affiliate of that company in Colorado. During this time, the original company, headquartered in San Francisco, was sold to another, much larger, company in New York City. I had been proposing a new entity of our combined companies—the San Francisco company and mine—and felt optimistic about our success. But the new owners from the New York company were much more corporate-minded than the former owners in San Francisco.

The new owners had a very tight structure in which to negotiate my compensation, and my original idea was a complete outlier to them. I was unprepared to renegotiate with so little information on what the New York company was trying to accomplish. When it came time to discuss a compensation package, I wanted to have a lot of latitude in setting up the new division, which would no longer be a separate entity, in Colorado. They wanted to set it up like a very traditional real estate company.

I asked for a dream about the new company and how to proceed with the process of negotiating a contract. During that time, I had been watching the TV series *Ozark*, which takes place where my family is from. I love visual symbols, so the *Ozark* format of providing intriguing hints as to what was about to happen in the episode intrigued me. Below is the dream, outlined in an augmented Problem-Solving Dream Cypher, along with my own illustration for the image in the dream.

The Ozark Way

...Something about an "O," like in the Ozark *TV series. It was a logo with four symbols contained in the O, just like the icon that appears at the beginning of every episode in the series. I then dreamed of four little vignettes that appeared as the story behind each of the four symbols.*

Write down the dream exactly as you remember it:

See the dream, The Ozark Way, detailed above.

Tell the story of your dream:

The first image was an ankle with a rash. In this part of the dream, some kind of germ was causing a rash to develop on people. I encountered it but hoped I wouldn't get it. I did. I looked down at my right ankle and it had a red rash, kind of like the grayscale rash in *Game of Thrones*, except this rash was red and curable, not gray, and lethal. It marked me, but it seemed like an ointment could cure it.

The second dream vignette featured a written message from a man asking me to join him on the boat. He was getting on the boat and asking me to get on the boat with him. He asked me to respond to his message quickly.

In the third vignette, I was in a tree with a group of people, and they invited me to join their picnic in the tree. They were all just meeting one another for the first time. I wanted to meet them as well. All were friendly and seemed part of a family.

The fourth was something about trying to get into a unisex bathroom. I apologized for going to the front of the line. I didn't want the people waiting in line to think I felt I was special.

Take note of action, direction, location, and timing:

The ankle is the part of the body that joins the foot with the leg—the gear to move from propulsion to action. I was marked by a rash because I hadn't yet created action. The direction wasn't indicated in the dream. The boat was in water that appeared to be the San Francisco Bay. The timing was current.

Describe the feeling-tone, and ignite your intuition:

The feeling-tone was one of adventure. I felt excited and successful—maybe a little hint of uncertain adventure.

List the symbols observed in your dream:

The four symbols were as follows: 1) an ankle with a mark on it, 2) a boat on a bay, 3) a unisex symbol of men and women, like you might find on a restroom door, and 4) a tree with people sitting in its branches. See the image I drew in my Dream Workbook above the dream, The Ozark Way.

Make a note of current and relevant life events:

I was negotiating a new contract with the corporation that acquired my previous joint venture partner. This corporation was much larger and quite a bit more formal in their negotiations and their structure.

Take a moment for a reality check:

So, let's analyze these symbols from my dream vignettes and contrast them with the current events. First, the rash on my ankle symbolized that I felt marked. I came into the company as part of a joint venture agreement with the original company—I am entrepreneurial and not an employee type, by nature and by contract, in this case. I negotiated strongly on my behalf, even writing my own contract. I felt marked because I didn't simply accept the first offer.

I believed I was viewed as a bit of a rebel because I didn't behave like an employee. I think I irritated the negotiating team a bit. Fortunately, the rash in my dream was not lethal and could be cured with an ointment—in other words, put a salve on the situation to smooth it out. However, I hadn't made any sales for either company so far. I suspected the management team wasn't sure I could do what I said I was going to do.

The second symbol was the boat. This particular dream vignette included the man in real life who had negotiated my previous contract. He was getting on a boat in the San Francisco Bay, where his company was located. His company had just been acquired, so he was embarking on the boat. Since I had several prior dreams that involved boats and work-life situations, I reviewed my history with the dream symbol of boats. When you keep track of the symbols in your dreams, you quickly understand what a symbol is conveying to you. Boats, to me, always involve business ventures. Will this venture work, support me, and not collapse? Think "lifeboat."

In the dream the man wanted me to call him back, to make a decision. The offer was on the table. Although, at the time of the dream, I had not yet received the offer. He wanted me to get on the boat with him.

The third dream icon was the tree with branches. The dream vignette was of a picnic where lots of people were perched in a large tree and having a good time. They felt like a family, and I wanted to be part of this family tree. The tree was, of course, the large organization being assembled—a blended family of related companies. The people were cheerful and friendly, as were the people at the new company. So, I was being told I would like them. That turned out to be true.

The fourth image was the unisex symbol, which is a funny insight my dream gave me. I didn't deliberately ask about the atmosphere of this new company, but remember, I felt it was much more corporate than I was used to. For twenty years, I had been a company owner versus an employee of a corporation. The unisex symbol had always seemed a bit off-putting to me. I felt that symbol typified sterility about a corporate atmosphere. It said to me, "Overly efficient and not that empathic." I couldn't imagine how this was going to manifest.

Here's how it manifested. My first day at work, lots of people were working at a long table and others were perched on couches-lots of noise and lots of distraction. I don't like working in an open environment. I prefer total quiet and privacy. I don't want to talk or feel like I'm being rude if I don't talk. I don't like to be around other people at all if I'm working on something that requires deep attention. I also like an engaging atmosphere. My workspace at home has always been filled with items that inspire me or delight my imagination.

As I walked to the back of this rather sterile office, I noticed the restrooms—unisex! Now I knew my dream was trying to reinforce that this wouldn't be my favorite atmosphere, but there were many other advantages to this situation. The scenarios showcased in the dream vignettes were clear about my circumstances.

Write a brief conclusion:

The advantages and disadvantages were obvious. Unisex bathrooms indicated I would find the corporate atmosphere to be sterile. I might need to work from home, an easy solution to the working environment. The mark on my leg represented my suspicion that there were doubts about whether I could do the work, presenting a challenge I might need to overcome. I needed to gain the trust of my fellow partners in this company, and this proved to be harder than I had thought. Still, I was being called to get on the boat. I liked the Founder and CEO of the original company, and he was encouraging me to join the team. The tree with people who were friendly showed me that I could become part of a corporate family tree.

Now make an action plan:

The advantages outweighed the disadvantages, so I knew I should sign the contract and get on with it. I decided to make a trip to New York and meet at corporate headquarters to get to know the officers better. I wanted to take full advantage of their vast resources. I was also cognizant I had been marked, so I couldn't forget I had a rash on my leg to overcome.

Give your dream a title:

O is for Ozark immediately came to mind. I later realized there was also an underpinning of things not appearing exactly as they are, just like in the *Ozark* series, so I changed the title to *The Ozark Way*.

See how that works? When you have dreams, or vignettes of dreams, that come in groups of three or four, decide if they are related and then enter all the dreams together on the Dream Cypher to analyze them as a set. In this case, since the circular icon came with four images, I knew the dreams were related. That is not always the case—sometimes you have a series of dreams that at first don't appear to be connected. However, such dreams typically entail some of the same symbols, people, or settings.

What if you don't know what the problem is?

What if, say, you are generally unhappy with a job situation or in your marriage but can't quite put your finger on the problem? If you haven't asked for a dream to solve a specific problem, you might get a series of dreams that elucidate the issues for you. The following example is from a friend who felt her husband was depressed, couldn't keep a job, and was hard to get along with. She wondered if she had married the right man. After fifteen years of marriage, she wasn't very happy.

I Am Still Married

...I was on a yacht and engaged to another man. I was leaving town, moving to another place and leaving everything behind. I was a duchess. I was very happy to be rich and have a yacht and a swimming pool. I wanted my soon-to-be ex-husband to pay one thousand dollars a month in child support. I wasn't sure that would work. I didn't like leaving my friends, the schools, or the house. I didn't know how my kids would feel about moving, either. I wasn't sure I wanted to leave everything behind.

I introduced myself to a group of people as Mrs. X, my married name. Someone said to me, "I thought you were divorced, but you introduced yourself as Mrs. X."

*I said, "I **am** Mrs. X. I am still married."*

This scenario dream was trying to illustrate to my friend that she had some unresolved fantasies. She wanted to be a rich duchess, in theory. She wanted at the same time to be married to her current husband, problems and all. She felt the fantasy of having a yacht and being rich would be fun, but she still identified with being married to her husband. She felt in the dream that she would be leaving everything.

This is not about marrying a duke and having money, nor about her future as a duchess—that's her particular fantasy. This dream is about her real choices and inner conflicts. I suggested she ask for a dream to clarify how she could have her best life. What did she need to know to have a wonderful life right now? She could identify issues in her marriage that led to her dreaming of a divorce and leaving town.

Money plays a part in my friend's dream. She dreamed of having a yacht and a swimming pool—a life free of financial pressure. However, her dream indicated that she still identified with being married to her husband. This dream gave her images of being married to a duke. She liked the affluence but not the divorce. That is the tipoff that she might not be happier with all that money.

Scenario dreams usually provide steps to understanding personal issues. Patience and self-reflection are two attributes we all could practice more.

CHAPTER SEVEN

PAST LIFE DREAMS

I have three daughters, and if I were to tell them of a past life dream, these are likely the responses I would get...

Oldest daughter: "Hmm. So, you had a dream about riding a horse with your hair—red hair, was it? —streaming out behind you. So, your hair was flying out behind you like a hot mess? Who were you? Someone famous, I hope. Where were you going? And why would you be riding a horse there? This probably isn't a past life dream at all. It's a problem-solving dream. Your dream is trying to tell you to switch to another stylist. Your hair is a bit of a fright, you know."

Middle daughter: "Oh, yes, I can see that. You would be riding a big white horse and have masses of red hair flying out behind you, like Joan of Arc. I totally get that. You were probably a warrior going into battle. That is so you. Hopefully, with a little better outcome than Joan's, right? Next time, remember to dream that you have a sword. Definitely, at least a sword."

Youngest daughter: "I don't believe in past lives. Be here now, I say. Hey, can you get those cookies out of the oven before they burn?"

If any of my daughters' comments resonate with you, that's understandable. Whether you believe in past lives, prefer to think of past life dreams as alternative life experiences, or just want to get to the actionable part of dream analysis, this chapter endeavors to put a commonsense patina to the usefulness of a past life dream. A past life dream is both dreamlike and practical. But on its surface, how can you tell if a dream is revisiting a past life or just spotlighting a personal fantasy?

I believe in past lives, and I've had quite a few dreams about some of mine. I find them insightful to promote my personal growth and to unravel my present difficulties. Past life dreams usually come with little fanfare. Unlike fantasy dreams, which often have lots of drama, I view past life dreams to be similar to character insight dreams.

Past Life dreams are frequently just snippets, not whole stories, about who you were and what you were doing in that lifetime. While a past life dream might come to you for various reasons, I start with examples of some that had practical present-life applications.

Here's the template for Past Life Dream Cypher:

PAST LIFE DREAM CYPHER TEMPLATE

Write down the dream and the date exactly as you remember it:

Tune in to the feeling first:

Tune in to the sense of the characters' personalities. What are they wearing? What are they doing?

Look for the shift in your perspective. You will feel a sense of close observation.

Look deeper and think again. What do you see in the dream character that reminds you of your current personality? Did you witness an unexpected trait or activity? Ask questions of the dream character: Who is this person? What can they help you with?

Note what is happening in your life right now that correlates to the dream insight:

Identify an insight you find useful in your life today:

Develop a plan to make practical use of an intuitive insight:

Give your dream a title and a date:

Past Lives to present life

In early 2004, I was running a company my husband and I started. The company marketed and sold resort real estate in the United States and Latin America. Projects had come flying through our door, and we were in a high growth phase of hiring personnel, expanding our services, finding new office space in the US, and opening offices in other countries. I was in the unfortunate position of having to lay off some employees who had helped us build the business, because they were not interested in or capable of contributing to its evolving international aspects. Our company suddenly needed international expertise and more sophisticated systems.

Our original team was used to being very informal, having few systems and even less oversight. I didn't think this format would work with our new clientele. We were now dealing with some very large Fortune 500 companies, not just local developers. I knew our company had to graduate to working with integrated IT systems. We needed to become a tech-savvy company, or we could otherwise lose our new clientele.

I felt misunderstood and disliked for making hard decisions regarding the staffing for the new business model. Even my husband wanted to keep the peace by not requiring people to ask for time off or to keep regular business hours. I had the following dream while deciding how to develop a company that could handle the tremendous opportunities that were crowding in the door.

The Judge

...I was a male judge, observing myself from the back of the room. The time frame was medieval-looking, and the man was dressed in all black. He had on a wig. His collar was ruffled and white on a black overgarment. The judge looked stern and unforgiving and was very proud of himself. He had very little compassion for others and didn't seem to feel their pain. I saw that he didn't seem to have friends or family who loved him. His loneliness stood out. He turned and walked out of the room. He was very tall.

My impressions were that I didn't like the judge very much, but I felt sorry for him. He was very lonely, kind of an Ebenezer Scrooge type of character. When I woke and wrote this down, I realized I tended to be judgmental in this life, feeling very justified in meting out firings and hirings without sufficient regard for my employees' feelings. I shielded myself from empathizing with them so I wouldn't be sad or reluctant to make decisions. This little snippet made me realize I had to adopt a better way to manage employees. I didn't want to turn back into that judge.

In this chapter I show you how to work with a past life dream, and how to distinguish it from an entertainment dream. Here's how to spot and decipher a past life dream:

Past Life Dream Cypher

Write down the dream exactly as you remember it:

See the above dream titled *The Judge*.

Tune in to the feeling-tone first:

The critical first step of deciphering a past life dream is to note its feeling. My feeling of the dream about the judge was one of observation. I didn't feel attached to the symbol of the judge or the man who was dressed in black. I saw the judge as a man I didn't recognize and didn't particularly care for. He had very distinct features. He was tall. He wore clothes that looked to be from another time—European, maybe English.

It's interesting that when I wrote down my dream, I wrote that I was a judge watching myself without much emotion. But when I started to analyze it, I realized I felt sorry for him. I empathized with him.

Tune in to the sense of the characters' personalities. What are they wearing? What are they doing?

Try to sense the personality of the dream characters to see if they have any connection to who you are now. This judge had a personality I didn't like. It was like viewing a film clip of Ebenezer Scrooge. The judge had on all black clothing. He was in an austere building, like a courthouse.

The primary hallmark of a past life dream is that you're observing the main character. There is usually a time frame outside of your memories or lifetime. This might include unfamiliar clothing or transportation. The dream with the judge took place in a setting that was several hundred years ago. The other factor to look for is that no other elements are familiar to you, including unfamiliar houses, people, pets, or landscapes. A past life dream usually comes to deliver insight or, as in my example, a cautionary tale to provide courage in this lifetime.

Look for the shift in your perspective. You will feel a sense of close observation.

Notice if there is a sense that you somehow know that person in the dream. Maybe you recognize personal traits from your present life, and sometimes, with a bit of surprise, you might relate to a character you don't even like much. You will very likely have a lucid sense of who you are now and a dream-like sense of the main character. Usually, you feel you have met this person before.

I found the Ebenezer Scrooge character to be endearing, in a way. Although a bit of a stiff, at heart, he was dedicated to helping others, albeit in a heavy-handed way.

Look deeper and think again. What do you see in the dream character that reminds you of your current personality? Did you witness an unexpected trait or activity? Ask questions of the dream character: Who is this person? What can they help you with?

When I went back into the memory of my dream, I sensed the judge was very concerned with the laws of the land and people's behavior. He felt responsible for the smooth running of the town and a proper business atmosphere for the townspeople's prosperity. I sensed his pride and an attitude of superiority over his fellow man. He was proud of following the rules and making sure others did so as well. In watching him. I also felt sympathy for his loneliness, his inability to reach out to others except in the context of meting out judgment.

I then realized I knew him. I didn't much like him, but I related to his feeling isolated because of his position. He was unable, because of his societal rules, to let emotion influence his judgments.

Note what is happening in your life right now that correlates to the dream insight:

I knew I needed to evolve my leadership skills in my current business. I was the cofounder and CEO, and I felt alone in making hard decisions about cash flow, expertise recruitment, and personnel reductions. I worried that if I were too emotional, my decision-making wouldn't be rational.

Instead of being open to the fear and pain of others, I closed off my emotions and was therefore regarded as aloof and uncaring. I wanted to unlearn some traits I had deemed necessary for good business decisions, realizing I could do both—be caring *and* business-minded.

Identify an insight you find useful in your life today:

I needed to combine both empathy and rationale for making appropriate decisions. The Judge could help with rational assessment of the facts, and who I am now could help temper that with care for my employees. I appreciated a learned ability to make objective decisions but added to my thinking that not all decisions should be made solely on rational thought.

Develop a plan to make practical use of an intuitive insight:

I decided to cater lunch for all our employees every Friday. We called it Phiroza Fridays, because we had an employee whose mother, Phiroza, was an outstanding cook of Indian cuisine.

Another employee was an amazing and witty cartoonist, so we started a company newsletter called *Communi-Chaos*, a spin on our company name—The Communiqué Group. The newsletter focused on making light of the company's explosive growth, with humorous insights into our projects, personnel, and clients.

It was a start. More important, I realized I could do better. I could be less rigid and more empathetic, even in times of chaos. Once I came to that realization, many other positive actions became easier for me.

Give your dream a title:

I chose to call that dream *"The Judge"*.

Here's another example of a past life dream:

Do What Must Be Done

...I was an indigenous woman, part of a tribe. We were being pursued by another tribe's men, who were very strong and

intent on taking us as prisoners. I was trying to escape with my children and an old woman, maybe my mother, in a canoe. I knew if they caught us they would kill my elderly mother and enslave my children. I would also become a slave or concubine. I wasn't sure I was strong enough to out-paddle them.

As they gained on us, I swung my paddle out of the water and deliberately knocked the old woman out of the boat. She screamed and quickly sank underwater. I knew she couldn't swim. I paddled on. I needed to lighten the load of the canoe to save my children. I didn't feel guilty. I knew she would have told me to do exactly what I did. I felt it was the only option to save my children and myself. I did it without a lot of thought—just an intention to do what must be done.

I had this dream in 2008, when I was going through a massive layoff at my company. I had worked so hard to build a staff of the right people, and the downturn in the economy meant I had to lay off all but the most essential. I didn't want to even go into work in the mornings. I could hardly stand to get out of bed. I gave severance pay to the first people I laid off. After a few months, the downturn became a full-fledged depression in the real estate market, and I realized I couldn't even keep the people I needed because I had spent our company's money on severance pay for the employees I had elected to let go. It was a sobering lesson.

Now, I really had a problem. I couldn't afford the staff I desperately needed to keep the business afloat. I had several warning dreams about the cash flow situation. Then, I had the dream about the tribal woman in the canoe. I knew I had to conserve cash and make very deep cuts in personnel.

Write down the dream exactly as you remember it:

See the above dream titled *Do What Must Be Done*.

Tune in to the feeling first:

My feeling was one of doing what had to be done for the greater good. At first, I was just an observer in the dream.

Tune in to the sense of the characters' personalities:

That woman in the canoe was resolute. She knew what had to be done, and she did it. She was intent on saving the children, who were the future of her tribe.

Look for the shift in your perspective:

I suddenly knew I had been that woman in a past life. I knew her thoughts. I felt how strong she was—her physical strength and fierce determination. I was intent on watching her and her activities. It felt like I was being drawn into a movie.

Look deeper, and think again:

Ask questions. What was that dream trying to tell me—that I could make very hard, even lifesaving, decisions? Fortunately, I didn't require such life-and-death decisions in terms of my business, but sometimes tough choices are necessary for the greater good, doing what is right for the situation overall. I had wanted to quit going in to work, to give up, before I had that dream. But I needed to save the business, for my family and for myself, and to do that I had to call on my inner strength. The dream reminded me that I have the strength of that tribal woman. It helped put my business issues into perspective. After all, I wasn't being called upon to knock my dear old mother into the lake. (You're welcome, Mom)

Note what is happening in your life right now that correlates to the dream insight:

Ask the person in your dream who they are and what they are trying to tell you. This is easier if you ask right after you wake from a dream, by closing your eyes and envisioning the dream again. While envisioning the dream, ask the person directly. If you are unable to get their attention, try again in a few days. Envision the dream, and then ask. Don't be discouraged if it doesn't work. Lucid dreaming is not a prerequisite for understanding your dreams. Relax, and pay attention to your other dreams. Also notice people who unexpectedly come into your life, or signs you perceive in your daily life.

Note what is happening in your life right now that correlates to the dream insight. Identify an insight you find useful in your life today:

I was not surprised to discover my past life as a tribal woman. I accepted it with equanimity. I could easily relate to her. I realized I was then and am now very capable of making hard decisions.

If on the other hand, you find you are nonplussed about or indifferent to the character in your dream, then see if you relate to the surroundings. Sometimes, a past life dream comes to remind you of a place you lived, to help you recall a feeling from a past life that is applicable to this lifetime.

Develop a plan to make practical use of an intuitive insight:

I didn't quit going to work. I let go of the office space, which was a huge expense, and asked remaining employees to work from home. In 2008, this was so revolutionary that MSNBC featured our company in a special report.

We got lucky and, with a minimal staff, landed a project that got us through for a few months. We were able to add back some staff several months later. That business rebounded well enough to get me to the next phase of my life. Now when I wonder if I have the courage to do something, I recall that dream.

Give your dream a title and a date:
Do What Must Be Done.

This is yet another past life dream I've experienced:

The Warrior in the Water

> *...I was a soldier—a large, dark man—in very heavy metal armor that looked Spanish. I was dying, or had died, in the tide on a beach. The tide was gently rolling me back and*

forth. It wasn't very deep where I was lying down in the water. It was dawn or early morning.

The armor had dragged the soldier to his death, because of his injuries and the heaviness of the metal. He had a very harsh countenance. His helmet was beside him in the water, rolling with the surf.

You might notice the proliferation of fighters in my dreams—a warrior type in times of struggle. In this life I am learning I don't have to fight to bring about my goals. Coincidently enough (and I don't believe in random coincidences), I was born the same day—October 2—as Mahatma Gandhi, the ultimate pacifist warrior. This is obviously a life lesson for me.

I am grateful I have had so many lives as a fighter—for justice as with the judge, or for survival like the tribal woman. Or even because, as in my dream of the unknown soldier lying dead in the ocean, that's what soldiers do. And, sometimes it doesn't end well. I'm also happy I have the wisdom of dreams to show me another way, so I don't have to take the hard path to accomplish my goals.

By the way, dreams are often humorous. They usually provide information that doesn't attempt to scare you about your present circumstances. They help you gain a better perspective on your current life. In my dream of the woman in a canoe, I immediately thought, *Good thing I don't have to make that kind of tough life-or-death decision today. By comparison, business decisions are easy.* My mother, too, is happy I don't have to make life-or-death decisions in this lifetime. Although, I notice she doesn't suggest visiting any lakes with me.

In summary

When you think you are dealing with a past life dream, ask yourself if there is a correlation in this life to what you were doing in the past life dream? What is the dream's main character trying to tell you? What advice are you in need of?

We'd all like to think we were queens or kings, or someone famous, in our past lives. However, my experience with dreams is that they help us in the current life, so you don't expect an on-demand dream about a life you wish you'd had. I've found dreams to be very practical. If a dream won't help you in this life, you might not get much information about a past life. Your dreams are meant to help you understand *this* life, which is your most important adventure. You are here to make this life wonderful, with the advantage of correcting past mistakes.

If past lives are of interest to you, ask before you go to sleep to see which past life is the most useful to you now. It might take several nights to receive a dream. Sometimes those dreams start as snippets, so don't discount those. Even if the snippet is very short or seems to show nothing of value, write it down. If you write down those snippets, you will get more information the next time. You will remember your dreams more completely as your practice deepens.

Dreams often work on several levels. They sometimes bring us experiences from past lives, current life observations, and suggestions for current problems—all at the same time. The next chapter, which addresses precognitive, prophetic, and visionary dreams, demonstrates how much information is available to you—not just from past lives, but right now in this life.

CHAPTER EIGHT

PRECOGNITIVE, PROPHETIC, AND VISIONARY DREAMS

Ralph Waldo Emerson was an American philosopher and a writer, credited with being the father of transcendentalism. His belief that we are one with the divine inspiration for the universe led him to believe strongly in the power of human intuition. He felt intuition should guide our actions and unite us with nature. He wrote beautifully about the human condition of lying in the lap of immense intelligence and being the receivers of its truth.

Precognitive dreams

Precognitive dreams are the baby brothers to prophetic dreams. We can use them to remind us not to misplace our keys, to avoid certain foods, or to make sure our actions match our interests. If you dream of losing your wallet with very little other symbology, then guard your wallet for a while. That's how precognitive dreams behave—short and to the point.

Once, I dreamed I saw my daughter, who was slightly turned away from me, in a doorway. When she turned around, I saw she was pregnant. I was elated and called her immediately upon waking. She had just begun to think about having a child but wasn't pregnant yet. Sure enough, within a month or so, she *was* pregnant.

A precognitive dream helps you with everyday problems, reminds you to call your mom, or suggests what your child needs. Don't take these dreams too seriously. They help you in little ways—remembering your keys, finding a lost pet, or reconnecting with friends are all small but real ways a precognitive dream can help. Your intuition is always working, even when you don't believe it or fail to pay attention. Most of the time, very few, if any, symbols are employed.

Precognitive dreams help coordinate your daily intuition with your nightly dreaming. They are very specific to your life. Just write them down—no need to use a Dream Cypher.

Prophetic dreams

Prophetic dreams are meant for larger groups of people—to educate or help them, or to expand the knowledge base of humanity. The dream Joseph interpreted for the Egyptian Pharaoh is an example of a prophetic dream. Harriet Tubman's dreams of escape routes for slaves to get to freedom are other samples. Prophetic dreams get a lot of attention because they bring about miraculous, unexpected events.

This is a specific template to use for prophetic dreams:

PROPHETIC DREAM CYPHER TEMPLATE

Write down the dream and the date down as you remember it:

Tell the story of your dream:

Take special note of the circumstances of the dream:

Describe the feeling-tone of the dream:

List the symbols observed in your dream:

Make note of current and relevant life events:

How does this affect you and those around you?

Is there a lesson to be learned or communicated to others?

Give your dream a title:

Here's an example of a prophetic dream.

Rogue Wave

...I was on a beach with several other people—mostly wealthy people I had known for years. We were having a picnic with champagne on the beach. It was a celebration, and everyone was talking about how good life was. Suddenly, an enormous wave washed over the beach and sucked away the table with the food and champagne. Nothing was spared. Everyone scrambled to find their belongings. Bundles of money were

floating about, sinking under the water, and then bobbing up.
No one knew what do. Houses were flooded and underwater.

Write down the dream exactly as you remember it.

Tell the story of your dream:

What is its story line? Let your storytelling skills embellish the small details so you can understand the dream's context.

Take special note of the circumstances of the dream:

What is happening, and who is involved? Is the dream's outcome positive or negative?

Describe the feeling-tone of the dream:

The prophetic dream will likely feel very different from any of your other dreams, even past life dreams. Such a dream feels like you are involved in an interesting fantasy production.

List the symbols observed in your dream:

The symbols in a prophetic dream are usually simple yet obvious, such as a car, train, or horse. It does not usually involve specific people, unless they are known to many and appear as a symbol of a larger concept. The symbols can apply to groups of people, modes of transportation, or atmospheric elements. Many times, storms or unusual weather are featured in this type of dream.

Make note of current and relevant life events:

Notice if the beginnings of the event in your dream have started in real life. Is the economy turning down? Are storms on the horizon? There is usually a concrete situation to which you can attach the dream, but not always. Sometimes, the prophetic dream just feels otherworldly. I know that doesn't help a lot, but there it is.

Now make an action plan:

While prophetic dreams seem to affect multitudes of people, there is usually a direct action to be taken. What can you do?

Give your dream a title and a date:
"Rogue Wave."

This dream occurred right before AIG declared bankruptcy. The recession started in 2008, around October, with the sub-prime meltdown and spread everywhere, unexpectedly. Money went up and down in value over a very short period. Many houses were considered underwater, worth less than what was owed on them.

Prophetic dreams help you become aware of impending crises, usually for the greater good of the people around you, in some cases, all of humanity.

Visionary dreams

You have read about famous personages having visionary dreams—Albert Einstein had them, and Nostradamus had them, as two examples. These dreams are distinctly different than dreams regarding your waking life issues. While you may think only famous people have visionary dreams, many of us experience them. They have an angelic patina about them, usually arriving at a turning point in our lives. They truly are gifts.

Anyone who has had a visionary dream knows how to recognize them. Rarely are they grandiose or filled with trumpets. On the contrary, visionary dreams tend to be a bit understated—but magnificent. Most of all, they feel very peaceful and unlikely to arouse strong emotions other than a sense of wonder or joy.

I've only ever had one vision dream. I recounted it in the foreword of this book. It was titled, "The God of Second Chances."

The main thing about that vision dream was it was so quietly powerful I knew to write it down as soon as possible.

When I was discharged from the hospital and returned home. I was still very weak, but I knew the vision-dream would be very important to me in the future. I wrote it down and the list of what I wanted, since I had been told by the doctor in my dream that I could have anything. I wrote the following:

- Perfect, healthy lungs
- Thick, beautiful hair
- Healthy body and skin
- Financial abundance
- Peaceful, loving relationships
- Creative endeavors that are fun, profitable, and helpful to others
- All of my debt paid off
- Voice and vocal cords in perfect condition
- A Lipizzaner horse
- A Ted Flowers Silver Parade Saddle

Okay, this was maybe not the most evolved list of things I've ever written down. Still, you get the point. There were a few more, but these wishes are to illustrate how I used the dream-vision. Those aspirations were written on April 11, 2020. I left the hospital on April 1.

I decided to use the dream-vision to manifest my desires, both long- and short-term. Some were simple desires, other more long-term physical wishes. My wish list has been satisfied on all accounts:

- I wished to be helpful to others. I didn't specify how, but I began writing this book with that thought in mind.
- My lung tests came back, and they were all very good. In fact, the doctor used the word "perfect."
- Soon after being out of the hospital, I began to lose my hair. That was a surprise. When my hair fell out, I bought a wig, which was thick and abundant. I realized I hadn't wished for my *own* thick, abundant hair. So, I amended my wish as such. It has taken about nine months, but my hair is growing back much thicker than it was before. (I prefer my own hair, but it was very nice always having good hair days with a wig!)
- All of my debt was paid off due to a generous gift.

- My voice and vocal cords are in excellent condition, in part because my middle daughter gave me voice lessons along with her choir. I had never thought of taking voice lessons or singing in a choir, and my voice was very hoarse due to being on a ventilator for so long. I feared vocal cord damage. When my daughter suggested I join her choir, I said, "But I can't sing." She informed me that the voice is just a muscle that gets stronger with specific use. She was right. My voice has gotten much stronger, and my vocal cords are undamaged.

- No, I didn't buy a Lipizzaner horse. I found one but decided against buying her. I liked the idea of having another horse much more than actually paying for another horse.

- No, I didn't buy a Ted Flowers Silver Parade saddle. I found one from a friend but haven't bought it—so far. I'm still eyeing it.

In both cases, when my wishes didn't come true, it was because I chose not to make them come true.

I don't have a template for the visionary dream. Just write it down. I have found the message of this kind of dream doesn't need analytics. You will feel its peace and abundance manifest in your life. You will feel you are part of a much larger picture than you formerly realized. As the quote from Ralph Waldo Emerson states, "We lie in the lap of immense intelligence."

As I have stated throughout this book, we can use our dreams for many purposes. That vision changed my life. I saw opportunities were all around me, even when I was in the ICU. I had a choice as to which path to follow and the God of Second Chances was there to help me.

Look for a peaceful feeling and a sense of imparted wisdom. Look for the threads of your destiny.

CHAPTER NINE

WARNING, WORRY, AND FEAR DREAMS

How many times have you said, "I knew it. I knew that was going to happen. Dang it." Maybe you missed all the signs leading up to a crisis. Or perhaps you didn't pursue a solution because you were too fearful of the consequences.

To evolve your decision-making skills, resolve to write down your warning dreams so you can be prepared to take quick action and avert more worrisome experiences. You know, the kind you wish, in retrospect, you could have skipped? Dreams of warnings, worries, or fears help you become a better problem solver, particularly around counterproductive thoughts or actions that induce these dreams.

The following chapters explore various warning dreams, worry dreams, and fear dreams, helping to distinguish between these three kinds of dreams. You can use the differences in these dreams to make better decisions more quickly, alleviate your fears, and relax your thinking. You will build an arsenal of tools to avoid or overcome negative influences in your life, in turn affecting others by not adding to the negativity.

There are two templates for this section. The Warning Dream Template and the Worry and Fear Dream Template.

Here is the sample of the Worry and Fears Dream Cypher Template:

CHAPTER TEN

WARNING DREAMS

"Beware the Ides of March," says the soothsayer.
Caesar asks, "What man is that?"
And Brutus, Caesar's loyal friend answers, "A soothsayer bids you,
beware the Ides of March."
"Aye, the Ides of March are come," says Caesar.
"Aye, but not gone," says the soothsayer.
—William Shakespeare, from the play, Julius Caesar

Specific warning dreams have feeling-tones that present dramatic or dangerous circumstances instead of the matter-of-fact feeling-tone of nonspecific warning dreams. Each of us likely has had some dramatic dream that warned of an impending disaster. Dreams of floods, fires, or car accidents are all warnings to be careful. In your waking life, pay attention to what you are doing that may bring harm to you or your loved ones. Many times, we are warned ahead of time to watch what we are doing. Literature is full of dreams that portended some unfortunate event, such as Julius Caesar and the Ides of March. He was warned but ignored the warning.

Warning dreams are usually very straightforward in their use of symbology. Notice the people in your dream. Is someone getting hurt? Are the other people helping or hurting? Do you recognize them?

Life's dilemmas sometimes stem from an incomplete or erroneous understanding of the actual problem. This chapter explains why insight into a problem is the front-runner of true problem-solving. Part of the answer relies on clear comprehension of the real problem.

Here's the Warning Dream Cypher Template:

WARNING DREAM CYPHER TEMPLATE

Write down the dream and the date exactly as you remember it:

Describe the feeling-tone of the dream. How did you feel about the actions that took place during the dream? Take note of actions, directions, locations, and timing.

Identify current life challenges that may be related to the dream, particularly anything that is bothering you right now.

What was the outcome in the dream? Were you, a friend, a relative, or a pet emotionally or physically hurt in any way?

Ignite your intuition, and see what associations come to mind. What can you do with the information you have been given?

Has your new insight into this dream helped you better recognize potential threats?

Give your dream a title that evokes the essence of the dream:

Here's a specific warning dream about a harmful individual:

Beware of Darkness

> *...I saw my cat perched on the side of a pond that had a beautiful waterfall at one end of it. He suddenly jumped in the water and swam toward the protruding rocks. He liked to swim, so I was concerned but not alarmed. A raccoon jumped in after him so quickly that I couldn't alert my cat to the danger. The raccoon grabbed my cat's neck in its mouth and snapped his neck. The raccoon proceeded to swim around in a circle, dragging my cat's body under the surface of the water but visible to me from above. The raccoon was showing off my dead cat and proud of the fact that I was horrified. I was so sad that I let my cat jump into the pond with a raccoon so intent on destruction.*

The cat in the dream represents my independent spirit. I adopted him as a feral kitty who was about to be euthanized. He was described as a "bite kitty." *Hah!* That's not the half of it. He is independent to the point of destruction—either my body parts or my furniture will suffer unless I let him have his way. I have learned to understand and live with this feisty creature. I admire him, in fact. For a fluffy little runt of a Maine Coon cat, he lives an adventuresome life.

So, for a raccoon to snap his neck and then drag him around the pond underwater in a victory lap was beyond cruel—it was sadistic, in my view. This dream was giving me the warning that someone in my life was waiting for me to swim in the pond with him so he could snap my neck, so to speak. This is how I interpreted it on the Warning Dream Cypher:

Write down the dream exactly as you remember it:

See the dream titled *Beware of Darkness*.

Describe the feeling-tone of the dream. How did you feel about the actions that took place during the dream? Take note of the actions, directions, locations, and timing.

I was upset at the image of my cat being dragged underwater and I was sad my cat was so abusively killed. I was also shocked the raccoon seemed to enjoy parading the dead body of my cat around. The raccoon really wanted me to be hurt.

Identify current life challenges that may be related to the dream, particularly anything that is bothering you right now.

The only incident that came to mind was a strange and very disturbing exchange with a thirtysomething young man who objected to his father's relationship with me. Instead of taking that up with his father, he insisted on talking to me privately. He lied to his father about what I said, then lied to me about what he said to his father. It led to some very confusing exchanges among the three of us. I didn't take him seriously because I couldn't believe an adult would really behave so childishly for so little apparent purpose.

What was the outcome in the dream? Were you, a friend, a relative, or a pet emotionally or physically hurt in any way?

My dream's outcome was the death of my favorite cat. I was emotionally disturbed by the cruelty the raccoon displayed. So, even though I didn't take it seriously when those real-life conversations happened, the dream told me the outcome was potentially serious—that it was a dangerous situation, really.

Ignite your intuition, and see what associations come to mind. What can you do with the information you have been given?

I thought about who or what the raccoon could symbolize in this dream. With a flash of insight, I realized the young man I described above had very dark brown eyes that reminded me of a raccoon's mask! He was very clever, always trading one acquired object for another so he could sell that object to another person in order to acquire something else. I had to laugh. He really did remind me of a racoon.

Note the word "mask," as in masquerade. This man certainly wore a mask, figuratively speaking. As for the symbol of my cat, he has always represented an independent spirit, which I value as a personal characteristic—although I'm not quite as independent as that cat, trust me.

Has your new insight into this dream helped you better recognize potential threats?

I now realize I had consistently underestimated the impact of other people's negative intentions. I pay much more attention now to others' actions. I don't swim in the proverbial pond with people I perceive as negative or emotionally abusive. I preserve my independence.

Give your dream a title that evokes the essence of the dream:

I chose the title *Beware of Darkness* as a reminder that people often portray who they are if you care to see. I always admired that young man's ingenuity but doubted his authenticity. However, I didn't see his cruelty until long after I met him.

Nonspecific worry dreams

What if you have a worrisome dream but don't know exactly what the dream refers to? Maybe you just feel uneasy about a business deal or relationship. Or perhaps you sense something is going on with your child, but you don't know what. Then, you receive a dream with a scenario that seems disturbing but doesn't have a clear-cut resolution. How do you solve a nonspecific problem? Let me give you an example of a dream from a young woman I know:

Panic Attack in the Forest

...I was in a park in a forest. It looked like an outdoor Las Vegas, very woodsy. My husband and son were there. We were watching a performance that involved birds, mostly owls, and other wildlife animals that were two feet to three feet tall. The weather was overcast. I didn't want the large owls to come near me. I was afraid of them and turned my back to them. One large owl in particular stared at me with cold eyes. He seemed angry with me. Every time I turned around, he was staring at me.

My girlfriend was making a tent out of sheets and bringing the animals into it. The animals, which included the large owls, didn't like the tent, and the volunteers for the show asked her to not bring the animals into the tent. My girlfriend was happy and cheerful.

I started having a full-blown panic attack. Everybody was having a good time, except for me. I was worried about feeling so panicked when others were not. I decided to walk away from the performance and have some time alone. A woman came over and put CBD cream on my neck. Another guy came over and wanted money. They were irritating. I wanted them to leave me alone. I went back to the show, and everyone had gone. My husband and son were also gone, but I easily found them by calling them on my cell phone. I felt very alone but happy to be reunited with my family.

What happened in this dream? There was no dangerous event that caused the young woman's panic. But the feeling-tone of this dream was one of worry and unease. To get to the core of this kind of nonspecific dream, use the same template from above. Then, wait to see if you have any follow-up dreams.

This may take a few dreams. Sometimes, you might receive

clearinghouse dreams to get rid of the worry that may be causing you to fret about an unspecified problem. Then, as a follow-up, a dream shows up with a situation to clarify your concern. In this young woman's case, she had a near-panic attack in the dream but no one else was bothered at all.

I asked if she saw something in her life as a problem that no one else seemed to think was problematic, she said her weight and dietary habits were of concern to her. She didn't like to talk about her dietary choices, and didn't want anyone with other opinions, even informed opinions, to try to influence her. An owl is usually a symbol of wisdom. The fact that owls were around her, and one seemed to actively dislike her, shows her rejection of and irritation about advice concerning her weight and diet. No one else was even aware of her concern.

The other young woman, a friend of hers who struggles with her weight as well, showed up in her dream as a symbol that this is a common problem within her social circle, but her friend in the dream was cheerful and happy. The nonspecific problem in waking life is this dreamer's weight and diet bother her but no one else, and she is not sure what to do about it. She doesn't like too many opinions, or owls, and turns her back to them. This dream is telling her to either enjoy her time with family and friends or seek out experts to help her. She is trapped in the middle right now.

My dream titled *Beware of Darkness* illuminated specific people who were detrimental to my well-being and happiness. The other dream, *Panic Attack in the Forest*, was advising a young woman to get to the bottom of the sense of unease she had despite being in a comfortable place with family and friends.

If the problem is still evolving, the solution path will also be not quite clear. Ask for clarity for the next few nights after having the initial dream. You will begin to dream about different aspects of the problem or worry.

CHAPTER ELEVEN

WORRY AND FEAR DREAMS

In the middle the night, it might be difficult to remember not to worry. That's when most fears and worries seem to attack—in the dark. But "Fear Is a Liar," says the Zach Williams song. Remember that.

Here's how to recognize and analyze—and evolve through—worry and fear dreams. I group these two types together because they are so similar. Aside from a nightmare, a fear dream feels much like a worry dream.

If the worry or fear dreams persist, ask for a solution dream—unless you already know the solution. If the issue is that you are reluctant to act, ask for a dream to reveal why you don't want to do what you know you should do. Most worry dreams just bring to the forefront your present life concerns. If you have had such a dream—and most of us have—act and stop worrying.

WORRY AND FEAR DREAM CYPHER TEMPLATE

Write down the dream and the date exactly as you remember it. Tell the story of your dream:

Describe the feeling-tone of the dream. How did you feel about the actions that took place during the dream? Take note of action, direction, location, and timing:

Identify current life challenges that may be related to the dream, particularly anything that is bothering you right now.

What was the outcome in the dream. Were you, a friend, a relative, or a pet emotionally or physically hurt in any way:

Ignite your intuition and see what associations come to mind. What can you do with the information you have been given?

Has your new insight into this dream helped you better recognize potential threats?

Give your dream a title and a date:

Here's an example of someone's worry dream:

Disorganized Jewelry

*...My jewelry box (my small one) was a mess, not organized
at all. All the jewelry was in a jumble in the top of the box.
I wanted to clean it up.*

Obviously, getting organized was of some concern to this dreamer.
Also, the jewelry box was her "small one." So, the organizational tasks were
minor in nature and not threatening. The symbol of jewelry means the
items had value to the dreamer, even if small. Jewelry represents personal
adornment, so the dream could refer to physical or spiritual care that is
disorganized and therefore ineffective. Or it might refer to the dreamer
failing to pay sufficient attention to someone close to her.

If you have a worry dream, assume a situational perspective and then
take steps to solve the problem. I advised this dreamer to look for areas in
her life that needed some organization. Had she forgotten to call friends
back, or perhaps not yet kept a promise made to family members? These are
just some examples of small areas of life that might be a bit disorganized.
But these small things actually are important to many people, including
this dreamer, as noted by the symbol of a jewelry box. Her dream was
urging her to take some small steps to align with personal goals, intentions,
or values.

Fear dreams

Many times, a fear dream is just that—a highlighting of fears so you
can resolve them. What does a fear dream feel like? And how do you
distinguish between a warning dream and a fear dream? In other words,
when is a dream a glimpse of the future and when is it just a baseless fear
of a possible future event? It sometimes is difficult to discern, particularly

when you have an emotional investment in a situation, such as a marriage or a job.

A fear dream usually has to do with a specific fear you have. For instance, if you are afraid of being lied to or cheated on because of a past experience, you might dream your husband is cheating on you. How do you know if your husband is, in fact, cheating or if you are just afraid it will happen?

Worry dreams usually have very low emotional impact, using a few symbols to get the point across. You might feel like you are watching a movie you aren't particularly engaged in. You might not recognize anyone or anything. You might feel warned or wary, but the dream does not take a heavy emotional toll on you.

Fear dreams, on the other hand, are very emotional—gripping and impactful. Ask yourself if the action in the dream is a very real fear of yours. If so, look for specifics that are familiar to you, such as real people, pets, or circumstances, rather than symbolic people, pets, or circumstances.

If you receive what you hope is a fear dream instead of a warning dream, ask for another dream to clarify. If you receive a dream that rephrases the first dream or involves the same people, places, or circumstances, you need to reevaluate the first dream. You are most likely being warned. Most warning dreams repeat themselves to drive home the message. Fear dreams typically don't repeat themselves.

After deciding on and decoding a fear dream, think about the specific fear that was illustrated to you.

Here is the Worry and Fear Dream Cypher Template:

WORRY AND FEAR DREAM CYPHER TEMPLATE

Write down the dream and the date exactly as you remember it:

Describe the feeling-tone of the dream. Remember that most worry or fear dreams are irritating instead of scary or highly emotional. How did you feel about the actions that took place during the dream? Did you feel uncomfortable or uneasy about the dream's outcome?

Have you had dreams like this before?

Identify current life events that may be related to the dream, particularly anything that is bothering you right now. If nothing in particular comes to mind, go back to the dream and analyze the actions in the dream. Do these actions annoy you or make you sad? If so, why?

What was the outcome in the dream? Were you, a friend, a relative, or a pet emotionally or physically hurt in any way?

Were there any symbols in the dream? What do they mean to you? Are they small or irritating? Important or not important? Remember most fear or worry dreams have symbols that incite a low level of fear or describe a worrisome event to the dreamer.

The key to recognizing a fear or worry dream is to assess how it makes you feel. Usually, irritation or sadness or anger, rarely is there much more to the dreams. Not much plot, not many symbols, not much insight to be gathered.

Has your new insight into this dream helped you better recognize your fears or worries?

Give your dream a title. Don't make it too dramatic.

Here's an example of a Fear Dream:

Afraid to Compete

> *...I was at a party or having a party. Someone had requested cornbread. I went out to get some and was eating pieces of it on the way back. Suddenly, I realized I had eaten most of it. I don't even like cornbread. Then, I realized I wasn't applying for grants or scholarships because I was afraid of not being good enough or smart enough. I was afraid to compete. I awoke, vowing to have more courage.*

Write down the dream exactly as you remember it:

See the dream detailed above.

Describe the feeling-tone of the dream. How did you feel about the actions that took place during the dream? Did you feel uncomfortable or uneasy about the dream's outcome?

I was uncomfortable the whole time, and I didn't see any reason to feel that way. I was at a party and having a good time. I didn't know why I would go out to get cornbread and then eat it.

Identify current life events that may be related to the dream, particularly anything that is bothering you right now:

I was about to go on my annual vacation with my ex-husband's family, and I was afraid of being rejected by them. I also felt I wasn't going anywhere, either career-wise or in building a solid emotional relationship with a partner.

What was the outcome in the dream? Were you, a friend, a relative, or a pet emotionally or physically hurt in any way?

No, I wasn't hurt. Nobody was hurt. I was just doing things I don't even enjoy, like eating cornbread. I wasn't asking for help to solve my problems in my waking life, because of my low self-esteem. I don't know why I would apply for a grant in the dream. I'm not in school. The dream's outcome was not bad, but I felt I was wasting my time because I was afraid to compete.

Ignite your intuition, and see what associations come to mind. What steps can you take based on the information you were given in the dream?

I suddenly realized I was feeling rejected on a lot of fronts in my waking life. I was not succeeding like I wanted to. I also realized I was feeling rejected, not because of others' actions toward me, but because of my internal thoughts. I was busy doing what others wanted and even eating foods I didn't like just to go along with the crowd. I wasn't getting on with my life's lessons for which I could get help. I can just act and not be so fearful. Nothing is holding me back.

Has your new insight into this dream helped you better recognize real-life threats or fears?

Yes, I hadn't realized my fearful thoughts were holding me back. Also, I realized I had access to help, not scholarships exactly, but sources of funds I could use to succeed.

Give your dream a title that evokes the essence of the dream:
"Afraid to Compete."

There you have it. A fear dream is a good dream to have, unearthing thoughts that are holding you back. The dream detailed above even held out the promise of funding. So, go for it. Dig up those fears and rid yourself of the negative thoughts that caused them. Even if the thoughts are lazy, background thoughts, stop worrying.

I'm pretty sure that enough has been written about worry to fill libraries. However, as general advice, I like this saying by guru Paramhansa Yogananda: "Sow the seeds of good habits in this soil and weed out worries and wrong actions of the past."

CHAPTER TWELVE

Soul Nourishment Dreams

Life is short, but it is wide.
—Mexican proverb

"That dream was definitely a soul nourishment dream," I said to my youngest daughter. "Those are very special dreams. They indicate how your life is unfolding before you, they are meant to encourage you along the way. I love that dream. Great job. I knew someday you would use and appreciate all the coaching I have given you on dreams."

"What coaching?" she responded.

Here, with my daughter's permission, is a fantastic dream about her path unfolding before her. It doesn't have a call to action, or any urgency to it, but instead a feeling-tone of peace. It reflects her deeply quiet, albeit sometimes sarcastic nature.

The Best Jeans Ever

...I was up in the mountains with another woman, who was a friend or relative of mine. I was giving her advice on decorating for a party. I remember orange decorations, like Halloween. Suddenly, I realized I was wearing the most wonderful pair of jeans ever. They were my all-time favorite

jeans. I love jeans, and these were the most perfect I had ever owned. I awoke very excited.

Soul Nourishment dreams are full of energy, insight, and feelings of peace. They sometimes come in a series because they interweave current circumstances with a broader view of how your life is unfolding. Many times, we are so caught up in our day-to-day circumstances that the progress we've made along our path is eclipsed by our focus on problems we need to solve—today.

While all dream types can be analyzed by using the basic template, there are some specific areas to focus on with a soul nourishment dream. Focus on the feeling-tone, and not so much on the current events or a reality check. Think deeply about what the dream pulls from your heart. In the dream above, being in the mountains with friends is one of my daughter's favorite activities. Jeans are her favorite article of clothing. The dream was hinting at a piece of wonderful news or an event around Halloween. She was being assured that her life was perfectly unfolding with grace and purpose, indicated by her assessment of this pair of jeans being "the most perfect ever."

Here is the Soul Nourishment Dream Cypher Template:

SOUL NOURISHMENT DREAM CYPHER TEMPLATE

Write down the dream and the date exactly as you remember it:

Tell the story of your dream:

Describe the feeling-tone of the dream:

List the symbols observed in your dream:

Review the past few years of your life:

Write a brief conclusion:

Give gratitude for having such a dream:

Give your dream a joyful title:

The symbols in a soul nourishment dream are crucial, not for what they portend or even represent, but more for the emblematic feelings they evoke. Mountains, to my daughter, represent peace and beauty. Jeans to her represent comfort, style, and grace. Her favorite circumstance on earth is to be in the mountains with her friends and family and wearing her jeans—her favorite pair of jeans, to be exact. The most relevant aspect of this dream was its feeling of deep peace and calm. "Good on yer," as the Irish say.

Here is another dream of soul nourishment:

Palace of Dreams

...I was with my horse Dublin, riding over to a palatial estate nearby. Dublin was walking perfectly through crowds of people, and she carefully walked over the slippery rocks of a waterfall to get to the beautiful palace. Brightly colored tents held food and were filled with people dressed in interesting clothes. Gardens and fountains were everywhere. I was directed to a beautiful suite in the palace, and Dublin was led off to a barn to rest and eat.

The Soul Nourishment Dream Cypher asks for a review of more than just current events. It asks you to plot the arc of your life to review the accomplishments you have brought about:

Write down the dream exactly as you remember it:

See the dream titled *Palace of Dreams*.

Tell the story of your dream:

Fill in the details that enchant you about the dream. In my dream, I felt like I was given a great gift with this horse. My horse was the epitome of grace, courage, and beauty. Everything was full of life and beauty. My horse walked around all obstacles with ease, as did I. I also walked with purpose and grace. It was a perfect moment in a wonderful life, full of interesting people and marked with abundance.

Describe the feeling-tone of the dream:

Did a feeling of peace and calm permeate this dream? That's the indication of a soul nourishment dream—nothing to solve. Yes, that was exactly the feeling in my dream—no stress, all obstacles easily surmounted, and all abundance laid out. My horse and I walked with ease and pleasure.

List the symbols observed in your dream:

Look for your favorite things in life. What do they mean to you? My horse is my favorite animal in the world. She represents my spirit. In my dream, she was an amazement to me and all who saw her, doing so much better at navigating a tricky terrain than I ever expected. I was filled with admiration and gratitude for her.

Review the past few years of your life:

What has changed? What accomplishments are you proud of? I survived COVID-19. I not only survived, but also thrived after being in ICU and on a ventilator. I gained financially. I saw, with a fresh perspective, how I could build a new life with a new partner and be a better friend and a better leader when that was called for. I began to appreciate my life as a gift. I accomplished building a bedrock of peace in my life. I felt like I had a second chance at a life I loved.

Write a brief conclusion:

Give yourself credit for solving problems, continuing your right actions, and eliminating bad habits. Write down these accomplishments so you can refer to them in times of confusion. Mine include an enhanced family dynamic, a better lifelong partner, and the possibility of financial gains.

Now make an action plan:

I vowed to be more appreciative of the people in my life—friends, family, and those I come into contact with. I also made note of the following:

- More self-discipline to accomplish whatever I want to
- Healthy heart and lungs
- Happy animals
- Beautiful surroundings
- All negative people no longer in my life

How do you appreciate the moments of your life? Ignite your intuition and see the connections between your daily actions and your dreams. When you have made those connections, look for specific actions that have led you more directly to your goals, and turn those actions into habits. When reviewing your path, perceive your feelings as guideposts to the life you want.

I realized that when I am relaxed and enjoying life, I instinctively make better choices that lead to self-satisfaction. When I try too hard, I make decisions that don't lead to more happiness, but instead to frustration or lethargy. When I do what inspires or fulfills me, I seem to have the energy to seek more inspiration and fulfillment.

Often, I too easily follow a path of "I must do this." I don't allow life to be fun, feeling it must be work-intensive. When life is flowing, I follow a more positive energy. I resolved after this dream to follow the energy of "want to," not the energy of "must."

Give your dream a title:

I chose *Palace of Dreams* as the title because everything was at hand in this dream.

Soul nourishment dreams can be slippery and pass by unnoticed. Take a moment to appreciate all the little steps that brought you to this point. It is not just your big goals and bold thoughts that weave your life into a pattern. It is the appreciation of small habits you've cultivated, small steps you've taken, and thought seedlings you've allowed to grow in your mind.

CHAPTER THIRTEEN

SOUL DAMAGE DREAMS

I've often wondered why soul damage is so prevalent yet not much is written about it. It is abuse of the worst kind. If you've ever had someone in your life who has betrayed you, lied to you, or otherwise caused you a great deal of emotional, physical, or mental harm, you've experienced soul damage. Don't blame yourself. We all have been cheated on by business partners, lied to by loved ones, or severely maligned by random acquaintances.

Why does this happen? There are so many possible reasons, for all parties. Lessons to be learned, lapses in judgment, and emotional patterns that need examining are all potential reasons soul damage might happen. We're human. Fortunately, our souls are aligned with our dreams. Dreams can be the bridge between your emotional self and your soul self. Soul damage is real, and as destructive as physical and emotional damage. It is deeper than emotional damage because it goes to the core of your being. It damages the one part of you that is foundational—your soul.

Soul damage is when another person causes you continued pain even when they know you are suffering. Think of the difference between your feelings being hurt, even badly once or twice, and losing the ability to feel at all. That is the difference between emotional abuse and soul damage. Soul damage causes you to doubt your feelings at first, then to deny them and finally to stop the pain, you might shut down all feeling. You might even forget what happened or downplay it. "It wasn't that bad," you might say to yourself, while behaving in ways that are out of character for you.

But what really happens is, to resolve the pain, you accept a creeping numbness in your heart. Drinking too much, working too much, overeating, being hurtful to loved ones, shutting loved ones out, or deluding yourself that what you see is not the truth—these are all ways you might vainly try to heal your soul. These tactics don't usually work.

What I've found works is a variety of activities based on better connecting with your soul and your purpose: seeing a counselor if that seems right, meditating, talking to very good friends, praying for solutions, and of course, asking for guidance from your dreams. Above all, acknowledge the truth of the situation so you can confidently act in alignment with your soul. This isn't always an easy path. It usually involves recognition of deleterious habits and some insightful self-discipline.

Be prepared to face such a period of time with courage. Your dreams never lie to you. Fear sometimes gets in the way, and you might have a dream that reflects that fear. For example, you dream your mate leaves you and you are heartbroken. This may be a fear you have, so you conjure up a dream about it. This dream might not represent the truth of the situation, but it is the truth of your fear. To further explore the difference between fear dreams and soul damage dreams, review the chapter titled "A Note on Warnings, Worries, and Fears."

Know that you will survive soul damage. The ultimate outcome is that your soul will sustain you by restoring your faith in who you are and what you are meant to do in this lifetime. The truth heals, and dreams can pave the way. Dreams bring stories that show the truth of a situation and people's true character. Let me be clear that the pain that inflicted upon oneself because a situation is not what it appears and the pain others knowingly cause are quite different.

The soul's certitude contributes to your emotional well-being. You are most connected to your soul when you dream, meditate, or pray—you can receive information from your soul that will keep you safe, point out opportunities, help loved ones, and provide the truth of any situation. When you engage in activities that involve your superconscious mind, you can receive guidance from a part of yourself that you don't usually access in the conscious state, except as flashes of intuition.

You can also communicate with that soul part of yourself when you dream. You can reassure your soul that you are following a better path, engaging in safer relationships, or protecting your health. When you receive a shocking blow to your self-esteem, as in getting fired unexpectedly, being lied to or deceived, or enduring abuse as a child, you might feel so deeply hurt that you relive the trauma for many years.

Usually, you can tell what part of you is being traumatized. We all have selves that manifest at different times. You have an identity from when you were young—were you an athlete then, or an artist? Then you have various selves as you mature, graduate from high school, marry, have children, or pursue a career. These selves are not just related to age. These are identities you manifest and sometimes shed when different circumstances arise in your life. If you lose a marriage, your children, or a job, you likely feel that as a loss of an identity. When this identity is central to you, soul damage might happen. Sometimes a person or situation in your life frightens or hurts you so much that a part of you runs away to hide. This also happens for those who experience a near-death event. Dreams can help heal this damage.

Here's the template for a Soul Damage Dream.

Let's look at some of these soul damage dreams and how to use the template to bring about solutions.

SOUL DAMAGE DREAM CYPHER TEMPLATE

The first step in recognizing a soul damage dream is to look for a child symbol:

Write down the dream, and the date, then ask for help in your future dreams:

Pay attention to the signs or symbols that come to you in the days following the dream:

Pause and think deeply on the dream, particularly if it seems to involve your well-being:

Look for a pattern of three dreams to illuminate soul damage and soul healing:

Use your inner magnifying glass, being aware of the dangerous elements in the dream:

Ask for and look for the solution or resolution dream:

This was a series of two dreams, dealing with the same soul-damage.

Young Girl and Cenote

> *...I was walking through a beautiful green pasture, holding the hand of a young girl. It was spring. She was about six or seven. She had curly blond hair and was a beautiful child. The child wanted to run ahead of me and over the hill that was right in front of us. I let go of her hand, and she ran off. I followed quickly and saw she had fallen into a cenote—a deep underground well of fresh water. Her hand reached out*

to me as she slipped beneath the water. I panicked. I was afraid to swim and afraid to dive into the cenote. I knew if I waited for help or ran to get help, she would drown. I awoke before deciding what to do.

This dreamer had another dream a few weeks later about the same little girl.

Same Young Girl and Elevator

...I was holding the hand of a little girl who had curly blond hair and was about six or seven. She didn't want to get into an elevator with me and, after arguing with her, I decided to get in the elevator by myself. As I was ascending in the elevator, I looked out its glass windows and saw that she was wandering off. I couldn't tell if some adults had taken her or if she was just walking by herself. I was terrified to lose her. I asked the elevator operator to let me off, but he said he couldn't, at least not for a few floors. After descending, I finally got off the elevator. I was not on the ground floor but a few floors above the main floor. I ran down the stairs to the main floor that led to the outside, but I couldn't find the child. I was heartbroken that I had left her. I felt I had made a terrible mistake.

This woman was going through a divorce and had just lost her job. She was also in a very emotionally unstable relationship with a new boyfriend. She told me she often vacationed in Mexico and those cenotes, usually found in the Yucatan, were a particular favorite of hers. She was impressed by their beauty but terrified to swim in them, as she wasn't a good swimmer and knew cenotes could be very deep. This woman was also a blonde, like the girl in her dream.

I told the dreamer this little girl was a symbol of her younger self. She lost that self, by being afraid to get into the cenote, "a deep underground well of water," which represented her fears about being deeply emotionally involved. She had let that trusting part of herself drown. In the dream, she hadn't decided what to do about saving the child.

I asked her what happened to her when she was six or seven. She told me her parents divorced when she was that age. She also stated her father had been very physically abusive to her mother. The woman had a vague memory of her mother covering up a black eye before accompanying her to school. She knew the incident happened when she was school age. So, she was maybe six or seven years old.

I told her the second dream was about her advancing in her career only to find she had left behind the caring child in her, who was apparently willing to emotionally commit, unattended. The woman got into the elevator without regard to where the elevator was going. The first thing to take note of was that she was not in charge. Someone else was in charge of when she could get off the elevator. The second insight is that the child did not want to get on the elevator. Maybe this career path was not what this woman really wanted to do with her life. When she was desperate to find that child, she couldn't get off on the right floor at the right time. She realized she "had made a terrible mistake." Not knowing where or when to get off the elevator indicated that she didn't know where or how to find that childlike part of herself.

So, how to begin?

The first step in recognizing a soul damage dream is to look for a child symbol:

Do you have dreams of situations in which a child needs your help? Soul damage dreams often feature children. Usually, those childlike images represent you. Sometimes, a child represents someone you are being asked to help, whether your child, a friend, or just someone in need. You will know.

I believe children feature so prominently in soul damage dreams because we are wired to protect babies or children—not to hurt them. So, children are a universal symbol for protecting what is very valuable to us.

Here is an example of using the template for Soul Damage Dreams to counteract the effects of soul damage.

Write down the dream, and then ask for help in your next dream:

If there is soul damage, the first thing to do is ask for help in your dreams. Every night for a week, ask for help with that child in your dream. Help will come. I believe that and have experienced it. Those of you who believe in prayer know its power is real, whether you are affiliated with a religion or just a practitioner of prayer. You will get a sign in your waking life, by a phone call a random meeting, or just an idea that comes to you. You might also get another dream that features a helper, or a fortuitous dream in which the child is happy or safe. Don't be alarmed if you don't get a dream right away. Soul damage has deep roots, so it might take a while. Whatever kind of help you get; it will be in your best interest.

Pay attention to the signs or symbols that come to you in the days following the dream:

Pay close attention to your daily life. What ideas or conversations do you have and with whom? What else do you notice? Do some activities or symbols become "sticky" to you? For example, do you suddenly see the same numbers everywhere, like license plates with series of fours on them? Or maybe you notice babies, bluebirds, or tall people are everywhere. It can be any kind of sighting, and it may not seem meaningful. Perhaps you dismiss the unusually large number of bluebirds you see but pause for a moment. The fact you are noticing them is a nudge from your subconscious to figure out what the symbol means to you.

Bluebirds are classic symbols of unexpected good fortune. When you see that symbol in a dream, it should encourage you to examine if you have a history of abundance or one of being left behind. Have you been abandoned in your life? Is the child in your dream lost or left behind? The bluebird symbol is a sign of hope for that child. Help is on the way. What—you feel overwhelmed by too many symbols? Then, follow the next step....

Pause and think deeply on the dream, particularly if it seems to involve your well-being:

Relax. Meditation is beneficial because it helps clear your mind. However, if you are not inclined to meditate, do something you enjoy. Take a walk. Clean out your closet. Go to an art museum. Take your friends out to lunch. Paint your bedroom. Draw. Do some activity that doesn't require much analysis. The goal is to keep the editor in your brain from weighing in on all the symbols you are seeing. The brain is programmed to analyze your environment and decide on the best answer to whatever question on which you are focusing but I would suggest refraining from analysis at this point.

Let the symbols rise out of a nonanalytical, nonjudgmental mindset. Don't ask if the data is right—just let it float into your mind, and then decide if it has any relevance to your life. Recognize any thoughts you have, even if they surprise you. Because soul damage is so unexpected, particularly if a person you love has betrayed you, take your time in noting dreams that are related to one another. Be calm and write down every detail—no matter how irrelevant it might seem at the time.

Look for a pattern of three dreams to illuminate soul damage and soul healing:

In many cases of soul damage, you will get a series of three dreams. You might get a dream of magnification—a dream in which you experience the seriousness of the damage. That is a message to take these experiences to heart. Then, you might get a dream that highlights an action step. Finally, you might get a dream of resolution. Notice how your dreams circle around a theme.

Use your inner magnifying glass, being aware of the dangerous elements in the dream:

Look closely at the dangerous elements. How are the symbols in each of the dreams interrelated? Remember, the first dream is usually the stage setting. The second might be further clarification of specific elements, and the third dream provides a solution or resolution. The second dream often provides potential solutions for you to act on right away.

How can you tell if a dream that comes to you a few days after the first magnification dream is the solution dream you were waiting for? A recurring symbol usually crops up to tip you off to a relationship between the dreams. Is there a child symbol in your second dream that comes to you after the first dream? Is there an animal that talks to you, or a disembodied voice that tells you what to do?

Ask for and look for the solution or resolution dream:

Solution dreams come about after you understand the real problem. Sometimes, these are daydreams that float into your mind and urge you to turn onto a street, or, in your waking life an old friend shows up on your doorstep. Like in the dream that follows, these dreams offer straightforward advice.

Let's look at a series of dreams that first magnified the soul damage, then presented a solution, and finally offered a healing resolution. First, here is the magnifying dream:

Alligator and Hippo

...I was walking toward a pond, leading my horse down to take a drink. A huge alligator rose up suddenly out of the pond and threatened to bite my horse. I was startled and was going to hit the alligator with a stick. I knew the alligator would drag my horse into the pond and kill her if he got her in his clutches. Just as I was about to strike the alligator, an enormous hippo rose up behind the alligator. I remembered hippos are the most dangerous of all wildlife in Africa because they are so vicious. I was now quite afraid and wanted to run away with my horse as fast as possible.

In the dream of leading the horse, which is usually a positive symbol, the alligator is a hidden threat. The pond is a symbol of emotional refreshment. When the alligator appears, the woman thinks she can defend herself and her horse with a stick, underestimating the danger. However, very soon, the real danger appears—the hippopotamus, which is not going to be deterred by a stick. This is emotionally very dangerous. This means the initial danger represented by an alligator, which most people consider dangerous, is surpassed by the more threatening image of a hippo—often considered the most dangerous animal in Africa.

So, two images are involved. The alligator is a sharp-toothed symbol of a creature that is not a friend to man. You might ask yourself, "Who in my life has sharp words for me"? Then, rising up from behind the alligator is the hippo, an even more dangerous creature. The next question you might ask yourself is, "Who in my life might be lurking behind the sharp-toothed person?" Both the alligator and the hippo were seen as male by the dreamer.

When asked those questions, the woman answered, "My ex-boyfriend is quite verbally abusive, and he has a son who has also been negatively vocal about our relationship." I told her the son is actually more dangerous than the father. Together, they have malicious intent toward her, at least verbally and probably emotionally.

I also pointed out that the pond looked idyllic in the dream, but if her wish was that her boyfriend would be a safe haven or an emotional respite, she should rethink that. Her spirit would likely not be refreshed from the pond.

Next came the intuitive action part. The day after the dream, someone suggested she listen to "Beware of Darkness," a George Harrison song. This suggestion came seemingly out of the blue and was unrelated to the trauma of her breakup with the boyfriend. The song lyrics seemed to be a warning. This was another sign that she was in emotional danger from the father and son. After putting it all together, the woman accepted that the dream and song recommendation were meant to enlighten her as to the danger she was facing.

Usually dreams, or insights of intuition, come in groups of three if the subject is of deep concern to your soul. The first dream is often an insight or magnification dream, so pay attention to its content. Usually, the situation is laid out with very little ambiguity, such as the dream of the alligator-and-hippo. Intuition brought the problem to the dreamer's immediate attention. Then came the suggestion that she listen to "Beware of Darkness." That song illuminated the situation she was in. Then came her resolution dream:

Little Boy Lost

...There was a flood, and I found a little boy on the front porch. He looked like the grandson of my ex-boyfriend. He was crying and lost. We were at a summer vacation home, and I wanted to make sure the boy was safe. I returned him to his family. Then, I returned to my family.

The solution in this dream was to return the child to his family for safety. The little boy was the soul image of the ex-boyfriend that the dreamer felt should return to his family. She felt the ex-boyfriend was mentally unstable and very hurtful to her, so he would be better off near his sons and grandsons. This dream of returning a little boy to his family was symbolic of letting an immature man seek comfort elsewhere. This is a positive approach that doesn't allow the negativity to spread. The woman who had the dream encouraged her ex-boyfriend to move closer to his family so he could see them more frequently.

Think deeply about possible solutions to the dilemma as presented by your dreams. I believe twenty minutes of meditation per day helps one concentrate and clears the mind of worry and fear. Whatever method you choose to still the mind, you will find clarity in that stillness and that is the real point. After or during meditation, take note of the thoughts that surface in your mind. Do you hear songs or envision images? Do people's faces or conversations waft through your conscious thoughts? Jot them down and dedicate a few minutes to ponder the connections.

After thinking about her series of dreams and intuition, the woman realized she no longer wanted any negativity from her ex-boyfriend. She wanted him to return to his family, and she didn't want any harm to come to her from his intention to attack her spirit, which the horse symbolized in her dream. The ex-boyfriend was very dangerous to her mental and emotional well-being. She had soul damage from previous experiences with former partners, and this particular partner intended to further harm her. She had been warned to "beware of darkness." The ex-boyfriend's move to another state was the perfect solution.

Healing resolution dreams come after you act. The third dream in a series is usually the resolution dream. It indicates that you have resolved the soul issue. Here is an example of another resolution dream from the same woman:

Horses and Snakes

...I was riding a horse, and a snake rose up to bite me. I grabbed it by its head and strangled it. It was a large snake, but I got rid of it. I was happy it couldn't hurt me anymore.

In this dream, the dreamer was on her horse again, and her decisive dealing with a large snake indicated that the problem was big. But she attacked its head, tackling it head-on. Notice the horse symbol reappeared in her dream.

She killed the snake in her dream by choking it instead of letting it kill her. This was a great dream about attacking the root of the problem, symbolized by grabbing the snake by the head. The dream indicates she no longer lets thoughts of harmful relationships invade her joyful ride through life.

As she reflected on this period of time, she saw that she hadn't believed she could be vulnerable to mental and emotional attacks—she had become numb. She believed if she didn't allow herself to fully love others, she would be safe. Knowing she could draw insight through her dreams, and avoid allowing others to damage her, brought her to realize she could fully love others with courage instead of fear. She became much more cognizant about who she associated with and how people treated her. She resolved to become more insightful and to act on those insights.

We are all going to run into people or situations that flummox us, hurt us, and even derail us. We sleep to heal our bodies and minds, and we dream to ensure we survive and thrive. damage

CHAPTER FOURTEEN

LIFE PATH DREAMS

I love the poem "A Noiseless Patient Spider" by Walt Whitman. He catches exactly the feeling of the seemingly slow, tortuous path taken through life day by day. Many times, we are so caught up in daily circumstances that the progress made along the path is eclipsed by the unrelenting focus on problems that need solving today.

Life path dreams are full of quiet energy, insight, and feelings of peace. They usually come in a series, interweaving current circumstances with a broader view of how your life is unfolding. These dreams urge you to look for the bridge between the events of your life, recent or past, and then take a longer perspective on the path you are following.

You may get a series of dreams that you determine to be other types of dreams, as well as a life path dream. That's to be expected. A life path dream usually is accompanied by other dreams to provide perspective on your present daily life, your future life, and a spiritual picture of your life.

Outlined below is the way to analyze a life path dream. The Life Path Dream Cypher is an abbreviated version of the Basic Dream Cypher:

LIFE PATH DREAM CYPHER TEMPLATE

Write down the dream and the date exactly as you remember it:

Tell the story of your dream:

Look for a strong sense of intuitive connection between your life events and the dream events:

List the symbols observed in your dream:

Make note of evolving life events:

Write a brief conclusion:

Find a deeper resolve:

Give your dream a title and a date:

Here's an example of one dream in a series of life path dreams:

Pink jasper Jewelry

...I was at an outdoor bazaar, like in those I visited in Belize. There were tables that had goods for sale. At one end of the table was a pile of jewelry—earrings and necklaces. I fidgeted through the pile, trying to find pink earrings in a heart shape. I found a necklace instead with heart-shaped stones. I had mistaken the necklace for earrings. I did find one earring, but its pink stone had gray streaks in it and other beads attached that I didn't like. I thought of stealing the earring as the table looked unattended, but a man showed up. He wanted to show me a much more elaborate necklace—also with pink stones, maybe Tibetan or Indian, and quite ornate. I wasn't sure I had the money or how much it might cost. Somehow the man meant for me to have it. As I awoke, the thought of jasper, the name of the stone, came to me.

NB: I looked up what the jasper stone symbolizes: I found that jasper is referred to as a stone representing physical strength and energy. It is also presumed to increase the stamina and endurance of life force in one's aura. jasper also brings the courage to face unpleasant tasks and to rectify unjust situations.

NB2: The depicted stone looked exactly like the image I drew in my Dream Workbook.

When I first wrote down the dream and analyzed it, I thought it meant I was to choose the lifestyle I want—the earrings meaning embellishment, or a necklace symbolizing a much deeper commitment. A necklace surrounds the neck, making it all-encompassing, and it is a much more substantial piece of jewelry than earrings.

Since jasper represents having the courage to rectify unfair situations or face unpleasant tasks, I thought the dream was about what it might cost me to pursue a lifestyle instead of a passion. I had considered stealing the earrings in the dream.

A few years later, as I was reviewing some dreams in my Dream Workbook, I came across the dream again, and here is the deeper dive:

NB3: I love jewelry. To me, it is the epitome of beauty and charm. So, it is a bit like having a wonderful life, symbolically. Also, the adornment of the self, is a symbol of the gifts of the soul as well. The dream was asking me to ponder what it would look like to have a wonderful life. The outdoor bazaar was a place of discovery—much like everyday life, right? We all have choices right in front of us, every day. The table was full of all kinds of jewelry. I was looking for a pair of heart-shaped earrings, which is a funny symbol. Maybe I was being shown that I was looking for love as an adornment and not a substantial commitment.

I found only one heart-shaped earring, not a pair, which is what is needed for a relationship. The earring had gray streaks and feathery parts that I didn't like. This part of the dream meant I wouldn't want the gray parts (depression, maybe) of the romance. I was not only choosing what kind of life or romance I wanted at this outdoor bazaar, but a man was also there to guide me in choosing something much more substantial than just a pair of earrings. He wanted me to have something elaborate—the beautiful necklace I was afraid I couldn't afford. Instead of stealing jewelry, the dream inferred I had help in obtaining this lifestyle and the beautifying of the spirit that the man revealed to me.

Who was this man in my dream? I later realized, after studying Paramhansa Yogananda for a few years, that his precepts have guided much of my current life. I also acknowledged I do have help—the gift of dreams—as we all do. This was a dream of life choices and how to make them—what to look for, how to look for it, and that it's unnecessary to "steal" it. This dream had much deeper consequences than I initially understood. I began to pursue some of my real-life dreams, such as writing a dream book, which I hadn't considered before.

Another example is a series of four different dream types, that taken together, comprise a Life Path dream sequence. I helped a young woman in the music business analyze the overall message of these dreams. These very special dreams illuminated her path, pointed out a specific problem related to achieving her life goal (or refining her life path), a possible outcome, and insight into her true self.

Notice the interrelatedness of the young woman's dreams. These dreams unfolded to reveal a suggestion for obtaining prosperity (scenario dream). This came through a vision of having rainbow highlights in her hair (soul nourishment dream), the frustrating obstacles in her way at the time (clearinghouse dream), and a possible outcome of her actions—living with a great kitchen over the long term (incubation dream).

I will walk through a Life Path dream series from writing it down to the analysis that follows to show how the dreams interact to inform the dreamer. This series of dreams was recounted to me in the first person, so I have duplicated it here exactly as she gave it to me.

Vibrant Rainbow Hair

...I looked in the mirror and saw my hair was a dull brown, but when the light shone on it, it was full of vibrant rainbow colors. I was very surprised to see how beautiful it was.

Frustrating Events

...I had a series of frustrating events—running out of time, having to go to the bathroom and realizing I didn't have time to find it, the bathroom being too far away, and a string not correctly fitting on my guitar for choir.

High School Theater Reimagined

...I was in my old theater in high school, and the set design was beautiful for a stage play—the musical Anything Goes, *which was not my favorite. But, surprisingly, a known actor, a star, was in it. I said I would see it if I could get tickets. I was surprised it was so well funded. I hadn't realized there was such funding and such demand for high school stage plays.*

Big, Beautiful Kitchen

...I walked into my house, and there was a big, beautiful kitchen with a center island. I never thought my wife and

I deserved such a kitchen. Yet, there it was. I almost wept with delight.

Tell the story of your dream:

Hair dream: There was a mirror, but I didn't recognize the location. I was surprised and elated to see I had such beautiful rainbow hair, even though at first I saw it as a dull brown.

Frustration dream: The choir I currently lead was the anchoring point of this dream. I felt I was too busy with choir, but I love choir, so I wasn't happy with the overriding thought of frustration in the dream.

Theater dream: I was back at high school, but the set was very well appointed, so I was of the opinion that it must also have been very well funded. I wondered if I could make money at writing stage plays. I somehow felt I had the opportunity to write stage plays for academic musicals. I realized there was quite a market for such musicals.

Kitchen dream: The kitchen was in my house—not the one I live in now, but one I just walked into and realized I owned. This was a big payoff for me and my wife. I knew she would love that kitchen. I never thought people like us could ever afford a kitchen like that.

Look for a strong sense of intuitive connection between your life events and the dream events:

Hair dream: I observed that I was mistaken about my hair. I need the light to shine on my hair. I need light, like in recognition, and particularly stage lights. I need to do what I do for a living—it sustains me.

Frustration dream: I feel I don't have enough time to accomplish bigger things because I have too many smaller things on my plate.

Theater dream: I was impressed by the funding, the set design, and even the talent in the high school play. In my waking life, I think better plays could be written and produced. I realized a bit later, after writing down my story about the dreams, that in another dream, songwriter Lin-Manuel Miranda said I wasn't "meant for Broadway." But I was quite successful in my stage play enterprise in the theater dream. I noted that I was surprised at rejecting his opinion. In fact, I had yet another dream that suggested a complementary line of work by which I could gain a lot of prosperity. In recounting my theater dream, I wrote about the market for high school and college musicals, "well-funded" was the term I used.

Kitchen dream: I owned a great kitchen in my dream. I was squealing with delight, and my wife was happy about it, too.

List the symbols observed in your dream:

Hair dream: I remember the rainbow symbol and thinking, *I have rainbow colors in my hair.* Hair represents my crowning glory, my creative efforts—I just have to look at it in a different light to see what I have accomplished.

Frustration dream: There weren't any symbols, just the day-to-day sense of being too busy.

Theater dream: No real symbols, just the storyline of being in a theater and realizing that community theaters were well-funded enterprises. This was a surprise to me.

Kitchen dream: Our family loves a kitchen—it's one of our favorite places to be. We feel it is the center of our house.

Make note of evolving life events:

Hair dream: I felt surprised and delighted to realize after this dream that what I do for a living is quite magical. Lin-Manuel Miranda had come to me in a previous dream in which he was critical about my prospect of getting on Broadway. I got that negative idea out of my head because I saw my hair was not just a dull brown color. I am now writing a musical. My musical interactions with others have become larger than I ever thought possible.

Frustration dream: Yep, I now see from the dream how much of my life has been filled with frustration and insufficient time, even for necessities.

Theater dream: I felt the amazement and potential of writing and producing stage plays, which I had never considered before. I noted the well-designed set and the star-quality talent.

Kitchen dream: As I said, I never believed we could have a great kitchen. In subsequent dreams, I was given direction about how to create this magic. So magic, relief, and amazement are the connections I feel for this dream—and even prosperity in the form of a great kitchen.

Write a brief conclusion:

There is more potential in my life than I had previously believed. The day-to-day rush of my life has kept me from seeing the great potential to both make money and broaden my creative abilities.

Find a deeper resolve:

I want to be grateful for the opportunities I have. I want to explore broader opportunities, and I want to have enough money to pursue my creative path without feeling a lack of financial resources.

Give your dream a title:
Vibrant Rainbow Hair; *Frustrating Events*; *High School Theater Reimagined*; and *Big, Beautiful Kitchen*

A mirror is a reflection, so this dreamer, in her hair dream, was seeing who she really is, which is bigger and brighter than she had believed. That's why we say things like "look in the mirror" to see the truth. Also, ancient wisdom was often given through scrying—looking into water as a mirror to see into the future.

In the Bible, God gave humanity a rainbow as a reminder of His promise to protect humankind. The rainbow-colored hair was a reminder that this dreamer has a destiny, a purpose. She is protected and is promised success. That's why she was given the symbol of a rainbow—not just shiny, abundant hair but rainbow hair!

The dull brown hair showed what this dreamer typically felt like from day to day, which is why she wasn't aware of the greater purpose of her creativity until the light shone on it. She observed that she was mistaken about her hair—her crowning glory. Also, rainbows are symbols of the unusual and magical, so she was being crowned with magic. Rainbows also have the ability to take ordinary light, like that which shines on hair, and turn it into something wonderful to behold. This is a fantastic symbol that shouldn't be underestimated. This dreamer could turn the ordinary into the extraordinary with her talents. Rainbows are also the symbol of the LGBTQ movement, which this dreamer passionately supports.

The young woman had made two significant comments to me: 1) She told me she had asked her dreams for advice on creativity, and 2) that she had some "home displacement" fears. She got lots of advice on both issues, including an indicated direction for success in the stage play business and a suggestion in the frustration dream not to overbook herself. Overall, she was being prompted to reexamine her "I might not be good enough" thoughts.

"Anything Goes" is a kind of funny aside because anything this woman writes might be better than that very dated play, which is not her favorite. She clearly has more magic within than she thought she had. Her last dream showcased the payoff—a big, beautiful kitchen! Prosperity and happiness are available for the dreamer and her wife. This is all a rebuttal of her prior thinking that she doesn't deserve prosperity.

I had an extensive phone conversation with this person. Over the course of the conversation, the storyline evolved as she talked a bit more about the dreams. I've heard lots of people's dreams, and when people first write them down and send them to me, I ask them to directly address the dream as if they are telling themselves the story of the dream. I might then ask questions: "What colors were in your rainbow hair?" or "Was your hair shiny?" or "Was your hair longer or shorter than it is currently?"

I always find there is more to the dream in the storytelling part than in the initial written version. Different parts of the brain are used when storytelling than in recounting. We edit things out for clarity when we recount, and we elaborate when we tell a story. Life path dreams are exquisite little mapmakers from which to navigate your life.

One last note: In 2024, the dreamer produced, wrote, and starred in a musical that was a sellout in her region of Ireland. She also moved into a big house with a great kitchen.

CHAPTER FIFTEEN

ENTERTAINMENT DREAMS

When you're lucky, your dreams take you on an odyssey—and what an adventure it can be. You might be flying without wings around a cathedral, chasing fish through the sky, skydiving from a trapeze, or climbing to a crystalline palace on a ledge above the roaring surf.

We read fiction for the purpose of expanding the entertainment value in our lives. Entertainment dreams provide that same sense of adventure in your dreaming life that reading a good book provides in your daily life.

These dream experiences are for your enjoyment, even if they can seem a bit daring. I don't use a template for these dreams. Just enjoy them. Here is a wonderful example of an entertainment dream:

Goddesses at Play

...I was with a team, and we had won a competition. We were asked to greet the losing team, so I headed over to shake their hands. I had on a flowing, lovely, shimmering dress. I looked radiant. I was on a horse, and the horse was behaving perfectly. I dismounted to shake the hands of the other team. As I walked through the crowd, I was amazed at how easily I could communicate with my horse. I had only to wave my hand or nod my head for her to move quietly around someone

154

or step gently over the roundish stones that guided us along our path.

We were headed over to a resort full of billowing tents, music, magnificent outdoor restaurants, and flowing waterfalls. The resort looked fantastical, filled with people dressed in unusual costumes. The architecture was not a type I was familiar with—otherworldly to say the least. I wanted to find a stable for my magnificent horse. I wanted her to be fed and cared for. I asked someone for directions, and she said, "Go to the goddesses. Just go to the goddesses." She was emphatic. I felt extraordinarily lucky to be there and knew I would have a wonderful time and my horse would be very well cared for.

Whatever you think of as an adventure or a brief respite from this life, your dreams will provide you with the entertainment you seek. There is no need for a deep analysis of an entertainment dream. If you awake feeling refreshed, excited, relaxed, or ebullient, that is what entertainment dreams do for you.

How do you recognize an entertainment dream? It is just like watching an entertaining movie. If you want to shout out, "That was fun!" as you get out of bed, that was an entertainment dream. If the dream features bad guys chasing you, bank heists, or unruly beasts eyeing you hungrily, that's fine, too. Not all entertainment dreams are full of flowing dresses and waterfalls. Car chases and underground tunnels can be fun as well.

Entertainment dreams can inspire you to take an unusual vacation, write a book, join a club, or just engage your creative fires to make your life more interesting.

Let go and see what depths of imaginings come to you in these dreams. Then, put them to work, if you like. Take a vacation, walk in the woods, or engage in that singing class. You will wake from an entertainment dream with a sense of how much more you really are—and that's exactly the purpose of dreaming.

CHAPTER SIXTEEN

CLEARINGHOUSE DREAMS

Clearinghouse dreams are just what you might imagine. When you have a lot on your mind, instead of illuminating an issue, your dreams are irritating and inconclusive. You might feel frustrated and think your dreams have taken you down a rabbit hole. They have—for a bit.

If you feel a nervous energy to your dreams for a few days, pause your analysis and ascertain if they are just dreams to clear your mind of worry, unfocused energy, or overpowering thoughts. I don't use a template for these dreams.

I recommend meditating for twenty minutes before bed, including breathing deeply for a few minutes before going to sleep. If you do not like to meditate, try one of many nighttime rituals to calm your mind: hot chamomile tea, deep breathing, warm baths, soothing music, no blue light.

Clearinghouse dreams are usually not very long, less detailed, and unlikely to stir up strong emotions. Here are some examples of clearinghouse dreams, which are untitled:

> ...*My in-laws didn't like me. I was upset.*

> ...*I was trying to get to work. I couldn't find my car, couldn't find the clothes I wanted to wear, and my boss was very upset with me.*

...I lost my car keys. I just couldn't find them.

...I was in line to get on a plane, but I missed the flight.

Not all dreams are created equal, and this type of dream is meant to declutter your mind and restore your equilibrium. This makes room for you to reconnect with useful information. So, how do you know when a snippet of a dream means something deeper for you to investigate—or is just a clearinghouse dream giving you the space to relax and recharge?

If the dream has symbols that feel "sticky" or interest you—say, an old car you owned when you were in high school, a favorite pet, or a house you grew up in—then, more than likely it is *not* a clearinghouse dream. If, on the other hand, the dream has very little to catch your interest, is not very detailed, and has a quite neutral feeling-tone, then it probably *is* a clearinghouse dream. If you are particularly stressed, you might have a few nights of clearinghouse dreams.

Don't spend a lot of time trying to dissect a dream that doesn't interest you. Your useful dreaming will be back when you are rested and ready.

CHAPTER SEVENTEEN

A Deeper Dive into Common Dream Types

I've yet to see any problem, however complicated, which
when you looked at it the right way didn't become still
more complicated.
—Poul Anderson, "Call Me Joe," *Astounding Science
Fiction* Magazine

Dreams can be very subtle. Sometimes, their deeper meanings don't
come to you until much later—hence, the necessity for writing down
your dreams. This chapter hopes to inspire you to look a little deeper
into dreams you thought you knew the meaning of. Like the witty Poul
Anderson quote above, dreams often reveal complexities you might not
notice the first time you analyze a dream. Dreams, when looked at from
a different perspective at a later time, can become more insightful—and
more complicated—because your story changes as you evolve, experience
more, and have more successes and failures.

Dreams have a sense of humor and symbology colored by the personality
of the dreamer and current perceptions of events that have transpired in
waking life. It's how we evolve. When we are ready to understand more,
we can review our dreams to see whatever we are ready to perceive.

Several types of dreams could use a deeper dive:

- Insight into Situations
- Incubation Dreams
- Scenario Dreaming
- Character Insight

For deeper understanding of dreams, you have had in the past, this template focuses on utilizing sharper intuition around the dream:

Deeper Dreaming Cypher Template

Write down the dream exactly as you remember it.

Tell yourself the story of the dream out loud. Remember and recite how you felt and what your thoughts were during this dream. How are they different now from when you first wrote them down?

What was the context of the dream? Is that still relevant in your life right now? If the answer is yes, what might you do now to change that dynamic?

What were the dream's main symbols?

What current life events might this dream be referring to? Have you asked for a solution? If so, review your question. Is the question still relevant? If so, what else do you pick up from the dream now?

Do a reality check, looking at past behaviors and circumstances that may have affected your perceptions. If you have a similar problem now, ask what you can see in the dream that might alter your perceptions of the issue.

Write a conclusion, looking at the outcome of the situation with an unemotional eye.

What is your intuition telling you? Let your intuition guide further reflection.

Give your dream a second title so you can summarize for yourself what the deeper dive into the dream infers.

Insight into Situations

Insight into situations depends on the maturity level of the dreamer and openness to an alternative understanding. When you later reread a dream, you may find obvious clues you somehow missed when first analyzing the dream.

I once had a dream about being on a descending plane with a luxurious coat on, which I detailed earlier in this book. In real life, I was worried about my job and if I would still have it after all of the layoffs were finished at the company. Now years later, I look more deeply at that dream. The symbol of being on a plane that was descending is much more noteworthy to me. I was never going to be prosperous from the job I held at the time, because the company was going down and not up. I should have taken it to heart that a descending plane is probably not a good prospect for continued prosperity. I was asking to get dream information about if I should expect a raise in salary and instead was getting information about a company that was not thriving. I also had a luxurious coat on in that dream. I now see I could have examined what prosperity meant to me. I might have realized from the dream that the company was a short-term solution to my long-term goal of prosperity.

I now see my desire to feel prosperous (the coat) is different from a desire to *be* prosperous. Asking what actions to take to move toward being prosperous would have been a better question, and the answer probably would have redirected my efforts to focus on a more direct route to solid prosperity. This would have been a good question: "What is currently the highest and best use of my talents?" The answer might have urged me to stay with the company or advised me to take a deeper look at my life path. My question, because of the way I phrased it, couldn't be answered most effectively. But the answer I got did save my finances and my aspirations in the short term. I would add an additional title to that dream, "What is Success?"

Incubation Dreams

To get additional answers from incubation dreams, just before sleep, re-read the incubation dream. Do this for several nights until you get a dream. If you remember even a snippet of a dream, record it. If, after a few nights, no dream comes to you, think about the question you have about the previous incubation dream and rephrase it. If any dream comes to you, even a seemingly unrelated dream, make a note of it. Answer the prompts on the template to see if the dream is a precursor to the information you requested. Sometimes deeper answers about incubation dreams illuminate further questions. Irritating, but necessary.

Follow your intuition. Those little pebbles will lead you to a solution, person, or bit of additional information you are searching for. This takes concentration and patience.

Scenario Dreaming

Scenario dreams provide steps to understanding issues that confound you. If you have had a scenario dream that doesn't quite make sense to you, yet you feel there is more useful information to be understood, read through your written version of it again. What has happened in your life that might change your perspective? Sometimes the scenario has changed sufficiently so that you just need a new set of scenario dreams, instead of trying to understand the old set.

Character Insight

This brings us to character insight, which is the trickiest part of dream analysis. How do you know if your bias prevents you from seeing a person's truth, or the truth about the situations and the context that influence the person's behavior? To start with, usually a dream is provided that outlines the context of the person's actions. Remember the dream I recounted about the young man urging me to rob a bank with him? Maybe he wouldn't be a trustworthy companion in the financial realm of life. But maybe he would be okay if you were lost in a forest? I recommend starting with the circumstances and going from there. Proceed with caution. And, keep doing a reality check.

In Conclusion

Be open to new perspectives on situations. That's the purpose of analyzing dreams—to glean additional information.

Be patient with the process of dreaming up solutions. The answers might take time to reveal themselves.

Ask the best questions you know how. Be aware that getting answers to your first questions can lead to better questions and then more answers.

When looking for character insight, pay attention to the behavior of the person in the context of the real-life circumstances. Try not to prejudge or emotionally judge the person. There is a lot of space for compassion in the process, as we are all travelers on this road.

CHAPTER EIGHTEEN

IGNITE YOUR INTUITION

What you seek is seeking you.
—Rumi

Now that you have a process in place and understand what dreams can do for your life, you can become a more astute dreamer and use the wisdom of your dreams to better steer your life. We all have that intuitive inner guide I call your Dream Sherpa.

Dream Sherpa:

This chapter is about integrating your intuition with your everyday life to help understand your dreams. The process is about developing your intuition like you might a muscle and allowing your intuition to have more of a voice in your everyday life. It's about listening to that soft quiet voice and acting on it.

Rational thinking is a wonderful thing. Intuitional thinking is also a gift. If you focus on a dream for just a few minutes, your Dream Sherpa will usually lead you to an idea, an intuition, or a response that you might not have gotten to following your logic. Try it.

163

Fractured fairy tales

Everyone has a fractured fairy tale—fractured because our dreams evolve as we do, along with the stories about our lives. Everyone has a vision in their head about how their existence should be—taller, shorter, richer, smarter, better appreciated, more attractive, healthier… you get the point.

Author Michael Lewis, in his book *The Premonition: A Pandemic Story*, has an insightful quote about this process: "Everyone has a story they tell themselves about themselves. Even if they don't explicitly acknowledge it, their minds are at work retelling or editing or updating a narrative that explains or excuses why they have spent their time on earth as they have."

In the process of weaving our stories, we hardwire our responses into these tales. We create the addenda to these stories of "must-dos," "should-dos," and "could-have-dones," usually accompanied by a scolding voice in the background that sounds very much like our own. We create our very own fractured fairy tales. Nothing seems to be working out quite the way we wanted.

What happens when your dreams indicate a different path than the one your life seems to be forging? How do you get back on the track? How do you get on that perfectly unfolding path? How do you find "what is seeking you"? Of course, this is the big question of life, and there are many ways to get to the answer. Dreams can help.

In this final chapter, I teach you how to dream better—how to more effectively use the advice from a dream by igniting your intuition so you can recognize and utilize its solutions and insight. This takes practice, so don't get frustrated if you don't get the technique down right away.

Dreams always sort out our perceptions of events and then update our inner narrative to reflect our newer perceptions. The inner wisdom of dreams provides answers to the current perception of problems as well as future insight when the time is right to discover it.

Here's the template I use for igniting intuition:

IGNITE YOUR INTUITION TEMPLATE

Focus on the issues you are trying to solve. Look for connections to what you see around you, what people tell you, and how you think about the issue.

Pay attention even if the dreams are just snippets—or particularly if they are snippets. Sometimes you need a slight shift in perspective, and a full-on dream might be overload.

If the snippets don't make sense, write down again the problem to be solved or resolved. Rephrase again for more clarity. Place the new request where you can see it frequently.

Wait until the next morning to see if any image, song phrases, or dreams arise.

Forgive yourself and others.

Practice letting your intuition have a say in your life.

Don't make it too hard.

Focus on the issues you are trying to solve. Look for connections to what you see around you, what people tell you, and how you think about the issue.

First, identify the problem you are trying to solve. Write it down with as much clarity as possible, and before you go to sleep, review your statement about the issue. Further clarify and restate the problem. Say what you want from the dream information—out loud if possible.

Pay attention even if the dreams are just snippets—or particularly if they are snippets. Sometimes you need a slight shift in perspective, and a full-on dream might be overload.

Be patient at this point. Pieces become parts, and parts become plans.

If the snippets don't make sense, write down again the problem to be solved or resolved. Rephrase again for more clarity. Place the new request where you can see it frequently.

Some people like to put writings or other items under their pillows. If this works for you, do it. I like to post what I've written in a spot that gets my attention. I'm always surprised by how much more insight comes to me as I see the written words or say them aloud.

Wait until the next morning to see if any images, song lyrics, or dreams arise.

Also, look in your waking life for any similar images to those in your dream or snippet. For example, you have a dream snippet with the image of a puppy, and you stop by a friend's house, and she has a new puppy. What does that friend have to tell you that you need to hear? Pay attention to those connections.

Forgive yourself and others.

Why is this significant at this point? Sometimes the issue is about a relationship with someone you love. You feel you've done all you can. The more guilt and anxiety you layer onto the situation, the more elusive the solution. This is when forgiveness can help—of yourself and others. This is sometimes the hardest part.

If someone has harmed you, it might be challenging to find it in yourself to overcome the pain. I also find it hard to forgive myself for my behavior, so I am not suggesting any of this is easy. However, it is necessary. To use your everyday intuition, you must have the mental and emotional space to examine and change your opinions of events and people—to amend your fractured fairy tale.

Your opinions of circumstances, people, or events determine your physical and emotional responses. When you forgive yourself and others, you make the space to change the emotional impact on your life and your future directives. This doesn't mean to quit looking for a solution. It means to wait for the right solution at the right time.

Practice letting your intuition have a say in your life.

Let those random thoughts have a voice. Write them down, or at least make a mental note of them. Review them and look for connections in your waking life. Take an alternate route while driving and see what comes up. For instance, did you intuitively avoid the traffic and spot a shop with exactly what you need?

Here's an example: I took my mom to the dentist, and the procedure didn't work as expected. It ended up causing her a great deal of pain. When we arrived back at her house, she was very discouraged and on the verge of tears. I left feeling sad and at a loss for what I could do to help. I feared my mother would go into depression, because we had waited more than eight months for her to get into the dentist's office for a procedure that didn't work.

I had to drive an hour, coincidentally, to my own dentist appointment on the same day. As I drove, I regretted my decision to make two same-day appointments so far away from each other. I felt I was far behind in my work and would need all weekend to catch up. I was less than cheerful at the thought. I drove the whole distance, grumbling about the waste of time.

When I arrived at the dentist's office, I grumpily apologized for being late and mentioned that I had just been to my mother's dentist. I described the issue and said I wished I knew what to do to help her. I was very crabby about the whole thing. The dental assistant exclaimed, "I have just the solution for you." She handed me the business card of a specialist for exactly what my mom needed. I wasn't even aware such a specialist was available. I realized in a flash there was a reason behind my decision to go to a dentist more than an hour away—so my mother could get the help she needed. The assistant called the specialist for me, and we had an appointment and a solution for my mother within two days. And it worked. She was ecstatic. I was ecstatic.

Don't make it too hard.

Many books have been written about lucid dreaming, being present in your dreams, or incubation dreams. In my experience, you don't have to put effort into trying to being about those dreams—they come naturally the more you apply your dream wisdom. Get the basics down first, and let your intuition become energized. The rest will follow.

Igniting your intuition takes a little time and trust. It won't be perfect. But given practice, it adds immensely to your life. You'll discover a peaceful blend of logic, knowledge, and intuition as you develop your skills. There's a place and a reason for all of your inherent talents in this lifetime. Your dreams provide innate wisdom to light your way. I hope I've enhanced your joyful journey.

If you would like help with your dreams, contact me at Michella@ yourdreamsherpa.com, or visit my website at *yourdreamsherpa.com.*

AFTERWORD

As soon as I finished this book, someone recounted to me a type of dream I have rarely heard or experienced. I was surprised. After many years of studying my dreams and helping others with their dreams, I had overlooked a dream type.

Spiritual Connection dreams come from deceased loved ones. I haven't had very many of them, but they are very powerful reminders of how important it is to spend your time with others creating strong emotional bonds.

Upon reflection, I realized the practicality of dreams doesn't and shouldn't preclude spiritual evolution. My strong focus on practicality had undervalued those little gifts of love and advice we get from those who have passed on.

Spiritual Connection Dreams

So, here it is. After loved ones have transitioned, they sometimes reach out through your dreams to help you. They bring lessons in the form of loving advice. They are blessings to you. You are very loved to have received these messages.

Here's my favorite dream of this kind.

A dear friend passed away on a beautiful Friday night in early September a few years ago. I had called and left a message to ask if he and his wife were up for a visit from me during the long weekend. They were known for having weekly get-togethers with their friends. We were invited every Wednesday, and everyone brought a potluck dish to share. I was fortunate enough to attend those dinners for more than thirty years. "Come for supper," Lawrence always said, enthusiastically. The day after leaving my message, I learned he had died that evening after going into the hospital the night before.

Ah, I had missed the last supper I would ever get to have with him. I reminisced about learning to ride a horse out on his ranch, to drive old International trucks (invariably missing a few gears), and to round up cattle for branding. I felt his passing was, indeed, an end of an era. I wished I could just have one last dinner with him. That evening, I had this dream:

Come for Supper

...Lawrence sat down across from me at his kitchen table. We were in his kitchen, just like we were for the many dinners we had together over the years. We just started talking the way we always did, about subjects we liked. We talked about books we were reading, our extraordinary horses, US politics, World War II spies, the Defenestration of Prague, and the complications of Russian history—typical topics for us! I was grateful to have one last dinner with him. My wish had been granted, and I knew it even in the dream. I told him so. "I'm so happy I got to talk with you one last time," I said. He smiled and nodded, then reached over to stroke my hand. It was peaceful, and he was content and healthy.

ACKNOWLEDGEMENTS

I have been lucky enough to have two strong women in my life who have helped me immensely.

Patricia Anne Narup, my mother, and Katherine Greer Clark, my mother-in-law.

My mother was a single mother in a time when it was notably not acceptable to be divorced and, in fact, was downright disdained. She had rightfully divorced a physically violent man and went on to make her own way with my siblings and me in tow.

She was a pathfinder as a young, single mother with limited means. She found good jobs, got a lot of promotions, worked in Japan for a few years, completed her college education, and paid for all of us to attend college. She never gave up. When life got tough, she just carried on, even when she didn't know what to do or how to do it.

I think I inherited, for better or worse, her dogged nature and indomitable drive. She paved the way for me and my siblings to become intrepid in our pursuits and creative in our endeavors. I thank her for raising the lantern of achievement and fueling my dreams. My mother is now ninety-four years old.

My mother-in-law, Katherine, known as Kitty to her family and friends, was a college professor and high school literature teacher. She is, hands down, the most well-read person I have ever known. She became a Canon of the Episcopal Church in her seventies, wrote and staged murder mysteries at eighty-six years old, and wrote her memoir at ninety-six. She is the most compassionate and wise person I know. Although I am her daughter-in-law, I have always felt as loved as if I were her daughter. Over the forty years I have known her, she has never criticized, never judged, and always encouraged all those who came her way. I have learned a great deal from her about faith and spiritual practicality. I credit much of my spiritual growth to her inspiration.

As I was finishing this book, Kitty had lunch with me and announced she didn't have many dreams but that she had one a few nights before. She recounted she dreamt that she had awakened out of a deep sleep and was surprised by a very bright light in her room:

The Choir

> *...In the light were my friends from church, and they were singing my favorite hymn, "Be Thou My Vision," and smiling at me. I wasn't afraid. I was sure this was heaven.*

She opined that she must have experienced heaven, the vision was so calming and wonderful. She told me she was not afraid of dying. She felt that after death, she would be reunited with former friends and her husband of many years—Forrest Clark, the love of her life.

I admire the fact that Kitty had a remarkable dream to ease any fears she might have had about death and dying. I wish for everyone to have such comfort from their dreams. Even if she hasn't had many dreams, this one was very special. Kitty is ninety-nine years old at this writing, remains active, continues to go to church, and still, a beacon of kindness and love for the whole family.

My three daughters are also very inspirational to me—all so different, all so adept at constructing lives that work very well whether they listen to their dreams or not (looking at you, Olivia!).

And now, for the men....

Tom Clark has been in my life, most of my life, in fact, as a friend, a husband, a business partner, and father to our children. I am sure I would be a very different person today without him and his continued presence. He has been the source of inspiration for many of my best ventures, particularly those that started out as ventures and turned into adventures, or misadventures depending on the timeframe.

And, to DC, who gave me hope and support when I most needed it. You changed my life, thank you.

Kelly White, in addition to being a super-smart editor and an extraordinary researcher with the eye of a detective, you are kind-hearted, while forcing me to be a better writer. Not an easy balance. The book cover was beautifully designed by Liz Driesbach, who managed to hit upon exactly what I was envisioning. My thanks and appreciation to you. The spot illustrations were done by Athena Lutton, whose whimsical approach brought a beautiful levity to the subject of dreaming.

And last, my heartfelt thanks to Richard Whitman, the first person to read and critique this book. His insights were invaluable, his suggestions, always on-point, and his background in philosophy helped frame and explain concepts that I struggled to illuminate in a dream context. He brought a higher level of rational spirituality to the book, so thank you, Richard for taking the time, it was an unexpected, much appreciated gift.

APPENDIX

The following pages include Dream Cypher templates for various dream types. Please note that templates are not provided for these four types of dreams, which do not require a Dream Cypher: 1) Precognitive Dreams, 2) Visionary Dreams, 3) Entertainment Dreams, and 4) Clearinghouse Dreams. By all means, write these dreams down in your Dream Journal.

A note on Precognitive dreams, Visionary dreams, Entertainment Dreams, and Clearinghouse dreams:

- Precognitive dreams are straight forward. Take care not to confuse these dreams with Fear Dreams. Refer to the Fear Dream Cypher for clarification.
- Visionary Dreams are so unique that you will awaken filled with awe. You will be guided on what to do. Trust yourself.
- Entertainment Dreams will do just that, entertain you. No need to overthink it.
- Clearinghouse dreams will likely be a jumble of irritating scenarios. Let them go.

If you have any questions about what kind of dream you are trying to analyze, the Basic Dream Cypher Template can be used to help clarify the dream type. Feel free to modify these templates if one of them has prompts that feel right for your dream.

BASIC DREAM CYPHER TEMPLATE

Write down the dream exactly as you remember it:

Tell the story of your dream by asking questions about the details of the symbols that were not in your first written version of the dream:

Take note of actions, directions, locations, and timing:

Describe the feeling-tone, and ignite your intuition by seeing if any thoughts come into your mind about this dream:

List the symbols observed in your dream:

Make note of current and relevant life events:

Take a moment for a reality check:

Write a brief conclusion:

If called for, make an action plan:

Give your dream a title and a date:

PROBLEM SOLVING DREAM CYPHER TEMPLATE

Write down your question, thinking about how to best frame the question:

Make notes of any issues associated with your question. Ask for dreams that offer insight about all of the facets of the issue:

Tell the story of your dream:

Describe the feeling-tone of the dream:

List the symbols observed in your dream:

Jot down current events, including signs you've recently noticed:

Do a reality check:

Write a brief conclusion by rewriting what the actual problem was and what the dream solutions seemed to indicate:

Make a potential action plan. What are your options-pros and cons:

Give your dream a title and a date:

PAST LIFE DREAM CYPHER TEMPLATE

Write down the dream and the date exactly as you remember it:

Tune in to the feeling first:

Tune in to the sense of the characters' personalities. What are they wearing? What are they doing?

Look for the shift in your perspective. You will feel a sense of close observation.

Look deeper and think again. What do you see in the dream character that reminds you of your current personality? Did you witness an unexpected trait or activity? Ask questions of the dream character: Who is this person? What can they help you with?

Note what is happening in your life right now that correlates to the dream insight:

Identify an insight you find useful in your life today:

Develop a plan to make practical use of an intuitive insight:

Give your dream a title:

PROPHETIC DREAM CYPHER TEMPLATE

Write down the dream and the date down as you remember it:

Tell the story of your dream:

Take special note of the circumstances of the dream:

Describe the feeling-tone of the dream:

List the symbols observed in your dream:

Make note of current and relevant life events:

How does this affect you and those around you?

Is there a lesson to be learned or communicated to others?

Give your dream a title:

WARNING DREAM CYPHER TEMPLATE

Write down the dream and the date exactly as you remember it:

Describe the feeling-tone of the dream. How did you feel about the actions that took place during the dream?

Identify current life challenges that may be related to the dream, particularly anything that is bothering you right now.

What was the outcome in the dream? Were you, a friend, a relative, or a pet emotionally or physically hurt in any way?

Ignite your intuition, and see what associations come to mind. What can you do with the information you have been given?

Has your new insight into this dream helped you better recognize potential threats?

Give your dream a title that evokes the essence of the dream:

WORRY AND FEAR DREAM CYPHER TEMPLATE

Write down the dream and the date exactly as you remember it:

Describe the feeling-tone of the dream. Remember that most worry or fear dreams are irritating instead of scary or highly emotional. How did you feel about the actions that took place during the dream? Did you feel uncomfortable or uneasy about the dream's outcome?

Have you had dreams like this before?

Identify current life events that may be related to the dream, particularly anything that is bothering you right now. If nothing in particular comes to mind, go back to the dream and analyze the actions in the dream. Do these actions annoy you or make you sad? If so, why?

What was the outcome in the dream? Were you, a friend, a relative, or a pet emotionally or physically hurt in any way?

Were there any symbols in the dream? What do they mean to you? Are they small or irritating? Important or not important? Remember most fear or worry dreams have symbols that incite a low level of fear or describe a worrisome event to the dreamer.

The key to recognizing a fear or worry dream is to assess how it makes you feel. Usually, irritation or sadness or anger, rarely is there much more to the dreams. Not much plot, not many symbols, not much insight to be gathered.

Has your new insight into this dream helped you better recognize your fears or worries?

Give your dream a title. Don't make it too dramatic.

SOUL NOURISHMENT DREAM CYPHER TEMPLATE

Write down the dream and the date exactly as you remember it:

Tell the story of your dream:

Describe the feeling-tone of the dream:

List the symbols observed in your dream:

Review the past few years of your life:

Write a brief conclusion:

Give gratitude for having such a dream:

Give your dream a joyful title:

SOUL DAMAGE DREAM CYPHER TEMPLATE

The first step in recognizing a soul damage dream is to look for a child symbol:

Write down the dream, and the date, then ask for help in your future dreams:

Pay attention to the signs or symbols that come to you in the days following the dream:

Pause and think deeply on the dream, particularly if it seems to involve your well-being:

Look for a pattern of three dreams to illuminate soul damage and soul healing:

Use your inner magnifying glass, being aware of the dangerous elements in the dream:

Ask for and look for the solution or resolution dream:

LIFE PATH DREAM CYPHER TEMPLATE

Write down the dream and the date exactly as you remember it:

Tell the story of your dream:

Look for a strong sense of intuitive connection between your life events and the dream events:

List the symbols observed in your dream:

Make note of evolving life events:

Write a brief conclusion:

Find a deeper resolve:

Give your dream a title:

DEEPER DREAMING CYPHER TEMPLATE

Write down the dream exactly as you remember it.

Tell yourself the story of the dream out loud. Remember and recite how you felt and what your thoughts were during this dream. How are they different now from when you first wrote them down?

What was the context of the dream? Is that still relevant in your life right now? If the answer is yes, what might you do now to change that dynamic?

What were the dream's main symbols?

What current life events might this dream be referring to? Have you asked for a solution? If so, review your question. Is the question still relevant? If so, what else do you pick up from the dream now?

Do a reality check, looking at past behaviors and circumstances that may have affected your perceptions. If you have a similar problem now, ask what you can see in the dream that might alter your perceptions of the issue.

Write a conclusion, looking at the outcome of the situation with an unemotional eye.

What is your intuition telling you? Let your intuition guide further reflection.

Give your dream a second title so you can summarize for yourself what the deeper dive into the dream infers.

IGNITE YOUR INTUITION TEMPLATE

Focus on the issues you are trying to solve. Look for connections to what you see around you, what people tell you, and how you think about the issue.

Pay attention even if the dreams are just snippets—or particularly if they are snippets. Sometimes you need a slight shift in perspective, and a full-on dream might be overload.

If the snippets don't make sense, write down again the problem to be solved or resolved. Rephrase again for more clarity. Place the new request where you can see it frequently.

Wait until the next morning to see if any image, song phrases, or dreams arise.

Forgive yourself and others.

Practice letting your intuition have a say in your life.

Don't make it too hard.

Printed in the United States
by Baker & Taylor Publisher Services